DINOSAUR MINIPEDIA

D0639680

tangerine
press

DINOSAUR
MINIPEDIA

CONSULTANT: PROFESSOR MICHAEL J. BENTON

tangerine
Press

TANGERINE PRESS and associated designs are trademarks of Scholastic Inc.

A Marshall Edition
Conceived, edited, and designed by Marshall Editions Ltd
Just House, 74 Shepherd's Bush Green
London W12 8QE, England
www.marshallpublishing.com

Copyright © 2002 Marshall Editions Developments Ltd

Scholastic and Tangerine Press and associated logos are
trademarks of Scholastic Inc.

Published by Tangerine press, an imprint of
Scholastic Inc.; 555 Broadway; New York; NY 10012

10 9 8 7 6 5 4 3 2 1

ISBN 0-439-38191-6

Originated in the U.K. by Grasmere Digital Printing
Printed and bound in Portugal by Printer Portuguesa

Consultant: Professor Michael J. Benton, Department of
Earth Sciences, University of Bristol, England

Designers: Nelupa Hussain and Steve Woosnam-Savage
Design Manager: Ralph Pitchford
Managing Editor: Kate Phelps
Art Director: Simon Webb
Editorial Director: Cynthia O'Brien
Assistant Editor: Elise See Tai
Proofreaders: Lindsay McTeague and Maggi McCormick
Picture Researcher: Zilda Tandy
DTP Manager: Ali Marshall
Production: Anna Pauletti

Pelecanimimus

Contents

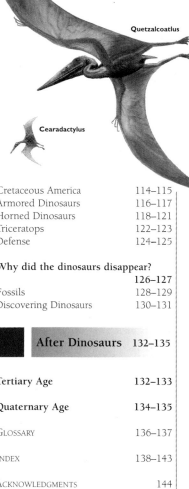
Quetzalcoatlus

Cearadactylus

Introduction

The Earth is about 4.6 billion years old. The first signs of life on our planet date back at least 3.5 billion years. This book looks at one of the most exciting times in the history of life on the Earth: the development of the first true land animals, the reptiles, and their most amazing representatives, the dinosaurs. Despite the fact that most of the creatures in this book became extinct millions of years before the first humans lived, dinosaurs and their relatives are among the most fascinating of all creatures. This encyclopedia brings them to life and presents them as the living, breathing animals they once were.

Our changing world

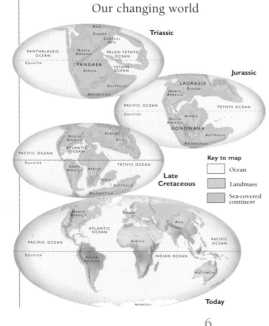

Triassic

- ASIA
- EUROPE
- CENTRAL ASIA
- PANTHALASSIC OCEAN
- NORTH AMERICA
- PALEO-TETHYS OCEAN
- EQUATOR
- PANGAEA
- AFRICA
- TETHYS OCEAN
- AUSTRALIA
- ANTARCTICA

Jurassic

- LAURASIA
- NORTH AMERICA
- EUROPE
- PACIFIC OCEAN
- TETHYS OCEAN
- EQUATOR
- SOUTH AMERICA
- AFRICA
- GONDWANA
- AUSTRALIA
- ANTARCTICA

- NORTH AMERICA
- EUROPE
- ASIA
- PACIFIC OCEAN
- ATLANTIC OCEAN
- EQUATOR
- SOUTH AMERICA
- AFRICA
- TETHYS OCEAN
- INDIA
- AUSTRALIA
- ANTARCTICA

Late Cretaceous

- NORTH AMERICA
- EUROPE
- ASIA
- ATLANTIC OCEAN
- PACIFIC OCEAN
- EQUATOR
- SOUTH AMERICA
- AFRICA
- INDIAN OCEAN
- AUSTRALIA
- ANTARCTICA

Today

Key to map

☐	Ocean
☐	Landmass
☐	Sea-covered continent

Plates colliding

Moving plate

Ocean

Remains of ocean

The moving plate carries a landmass

As the plates crash together, the ocean sediments are pushed up

Ocean sediments

▲The surface of the Earth is divided into a number of sections called plates. These are constantly on the move, carrying the world's landmasses with them. Over millions of years, this can change the shape of continents as happened during the time of the dinosaurs. When one plate collides with another, land and ocean sediments can be pushed up, creating a mountain range.

◄This series of maps shows how the shape of the Earth's landmasses has changed over millions of years. During the Triassic period, when dinosaurs first appeared, most of the world's land formed one supercontinent called Pangaea. During the Jurassic period, Pangaea started to split apart, forming northern and southern landmasses. By the Late Cretaceous period, these had subdivided further and began to take the shape of the continents we know today.

▶The history of the Earth is divided into two major eons: the Precambrian and the Phanerozoic. The Precambrian is the largest, spanning the time from the Earth's origins to the beginnings of life. The Phanerozoic dates from the time when life began to thrive on the Earth and includes three eras: the Paleozoic, Mesozoic, and Cenozoic. These are in turn divided into periods and epochs. The dates on the chart (right) show how many millions of years ago (mya) each began.

How to use this book

This encyclopedia is divided into two chapters: early reptiles and dinosaurs. Each chapter contains an introduction, a description of what makes a reptile or a dinosaur, illustrations of and facts about different species, and focus pages that look in more detail at particular topics. There are also special double-page features on the three periods in the age of the dinosaurs—the Triassic, Jurassic, and Cretaceous—and one on why dinosaurs disappeared.

Ocean sediments

Folding

Mountain range

Faulting

Collision of the plates causes a mountain range to form

Scale
The silhouettes compare the size of the animal with an average adult human.

Period
The symbols show the periods in which the animals lived. The key is below.

Size
The approximate size of the animal is given in imperial and metric measurements. See page 143 for a list of the abbreviations in the book.

Order
This gives the order to which the family belongs (see pages 12–13 and 56–57).

Family
This gives the family to which the species belongs (see pages 12–13 and 56–57).

Range
This lists the areas of the world in which fossils of the species have been found.

Pn (Pronunciation)
This lists how to say the animal's name. Capital letters (AM) show that this part of the word should be stressed.

Siamotyrannus

Cr Early Cretaceous

Size: 16–23 ft. (5–7 m) long
Order: Saurischia
Family: Tyrannosauridae
Range: Asia: Thailand
Pn: sigh-AM-oh-TIE-ran-us

Period chart

Eon	Era	Period	Epoch	Date at beginning (mya)
Phanerozoic eon				
	Cenozoic era			
		Quaternary period		
			Holocene epoch	0.01
			Pleistocene epoch	1.6
		Tertiary period		
			Pliocene epoch	5
			Miocene epoch	23
			Oligocene epoch	35
			Eocene epoch	56
			Paleocene epoch	65
	Mesozoic era			
		Cretaceous period		146
		Jurassic period		208
		Triassic period		250
	Paleozoic era			
		Permian period		290
		Carboniferous period		362
		Devonian period		408
		Silurian period		439
		Ordovician period		510
		Cambrian period		550
Precambrian				4,560

Key to symbols

Ca Carboniferous
362 to 290 mya

P Permian
290 to 250 mya

T Triassic
250 to 208 mya

J Jurassic
208 to 146 mya

Cr Cretaceous
146 to 65 mya

Pa Paleocene
65 to 56 mya

Pli Pliocene
5 to 1.6 mya

Ple Pleistocene
1.6 mya to 10,000 years ago

7

Early Reptiles

Reptiles today include animals such as turtles, crocodiles, lizards, and snakes. All have a bony skeleton and scaly skin, and most lay eggs. Although turtles and a few other kinds of reptiles live in water, most spend their lives on land.

In prehistoric times there were many kinds of reptiles not found today. The first reptiles, which lived 100 million years before the dinosaurs, were small lizardlike creatures. Later, at the time of the dinosaurs, came the flying reptiles called pterosaurs and the many kinds of marine reptiles such as ichthyosaurs and plesiosaurs. Another important group included the mammal-like reptiles, which dominated life on the Earth before the dinosaurs, but died out by the end of the Jurassic period. The most complex of these reptiles were the ancestors of the mammals, the group to which humans belong.

This fossilized skull belonged to a flying reptile called **Scaphognathus**, which lived in Europe during the Jurassic period. It probably fed on fish, swooping down to snatch its prey from the water with its long jaws.

Longisquama

9

What were the early reptiles?

Reptiles developed from amphibians and were the first true land vertebrates (animals with backbones). Amphibians generally lay their eggs in water and spend the first part of their lives there. The great advance of the reptiles was that they had an egg with a shell that did not dry out in air and could be laid on dry land, so freeing them from their dependence on water. After the appearance of the first reptiles in the Late Carboniferous, different types of reptiles began to spread all over the world. At the same time, marine forms such as plesiosaurs and ichthyosaurs were beginning to thrive in the sea. Crocodiles and flying reptiles belonged to the archosaur or "ruling reptile" group, as did the dinosaurs. Of these, only crocodiles remain today.

Shell

Reptile egg

Amphibian egg

Jelly

Embryo

Embryo

A shelled egg

An amphibian egg is protected only by a jelly coating. The egg of a reptile is protected by a tough shell, which keeps the developing baby, called an embryo, from drying out. It also protects it from predators.

An early reptile

One of the first reptiles and earliest of all land vertebrates, *Hylonomus* was a lightly built, lizardlike creature. Its jaws were more powerful than those of its amphibian ancestors and its hips and shoulders were stronger to help support it on land.

Long bony tail

SKELETON OF A HYLONOMUS

Boxlike head

Ribcage with 26 vertebrae

Five-fingered hand

Slender five-toed foot

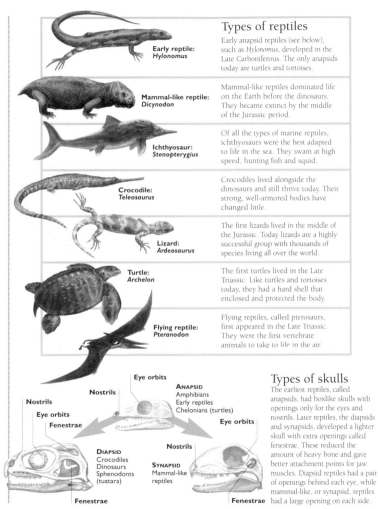

Types of reptiles

Early anapsid reptiles (see below), such as *Hylonomus*, developed in the Late Carboniferous. The only anapsids today are turtles and tortoises.

Early reptile:
Hylonomus

Mammal-like reptiles dominated life on the Earth before the dinosaurs. They became extinct by the middle of the Jurassic period.

Mammal-like reptile:
Dicynodon

Of all the types of marine reptiles, ichthyosaurs were the best adapted to life in the sea. They swam at high speed, hunting fish and squid.

Ichthyosaur:
Stenopterygius

Crocodiles lived alongside the dinosaurs and still thrive today. Their strong, well-armored bodies have changed little.

Crocodile:
Teleosaurus

The first lizards lived in the middle of the Jurassic. Today lizards are a highly successful group with thousands of species living all over the world.

Lizard:
Ardeosaurus

The first turtles lived in the Late Triassic. Like turtles and tortoises today, they had a hard shell that enclosed and protected the body.

Turtle:
Archelon

Flying reptiles, called pterosaurs, first appeared in the Late Triassic. They were the first vertebrate animals to take to life in the air.

Flying reptile:
Pteranodon

Types of skulls

The earliest reptiles, called anapsids, had boxlike skulls with openings only for the eyes and nostrils. Later reptiles, the diapsids and synapsids, developed a lighter skull with extra openings called fenestrae. These reduced the amount of heavy bone and gave better attachment points for jaw muscles. Diapsid reptiles had a pair of openings behind each eye, while mammal-like, or synapsid, reptiles had a large opening on each side.

ANAPSID
Amphibians
Early reptiles
Chelonians (turtles)

Eye orbits
Nostrils

DIAPSID
Crocodiles
Dinosaurs
Sphenodonts
(tuatara)

Nostrils
Eye orbits
Fenestrae
Fenestrae

SYNAPSID
Mammal-like
reptiles

Nostrils
Eye orbits
Fenestrae

A Reptile Family Tree

The first reptiles, which appeared in the Late Carboniferous, were the primitive anapsids, still represented today by tortoises and turtles. They gave rise to the synapsid reptiles, the ancestors of the mammals, and to the diapsid reptiles, which later included dinosaurs as well as modern lizards and snakes. Many of these groups of reptiles are now extinct.

Reptile groups

Animals are classified into groups of different sizes. The smallest is the species, and every species is contained in a genus (plural, genera). So for Pterodactylus kochi, kochi is the species name and Pterodactylus the genus. All genera are classified into families, families into suborders, suborders into orders, and so on.

REPTILES

SYNAPSIDA

ANAPSIDA

DIAPSIDA

ARCHOSAUR-OMORPHA

The chart

At the far right of the chart the names ending in "idae" are all families, which contain a number of closely related species of reptiles. Names ending in "ia" or "formes" are larger groups, containing a number of families. Names in capital letters are of major groups such as mammals and dinosaurs. The orders and suborders (such as Archosauria) in the book are also labeled.

Two **paleontologists** work on a reconstructed skeleton of a plesiosaur, a type of marine reptile common at the time of the dinosaurs. Experts have long argued about how these reptiles moved. At first, they thought that they beat their paddlelike flippers backwards and forwards like oars. Now most agree that plesiosaurs moved their flippers in a figure-eight shape as though flying through the water.

12

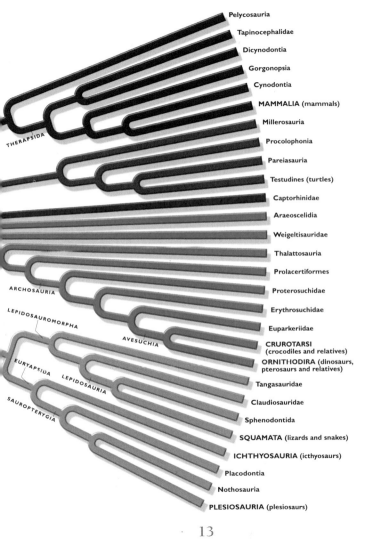

Pelycosauria

Tapinocephalidae

Dicynodontia

Gorgonopsia

Cynodontia

MAMMALIA (mammals)

Millerosauria

Procolophonia

Pareiasauria

Testudines (turtles)

Captorhinidae

Araeoscelidia

Weigeltisauridae

Thalattosauria

Prolacertiformes

Proterosuchidae

Erythrosuchidae

Euparkeriidae

CRUROTARSI
(crocodiles and relatives)

ORNITHODIRA (dinosaurs,
pterosaurs and relatives)

Tangasauridae

Claudiosauridae

Sphenodontida

SQUAMATA (lizards and snakes)

ICHTHYOSAURIA (icthyosaurs)

Placodontia

Nothosauria

PLESIOSAURIA (plesiosaurs)

THERAPSIDA

ARCHOSAURIA

LEPIDOSAUROMORPHA

AVESUCHIA

EURYAPSIDA

LEPIDOSAURIA

SAUROPTERYGIA

The First Reptiles

Reptiles evolved during the Late Carboniferous period about 300 million years ago. Many groups thrived before the archosaurs, or ruling reptiles, which included dinosaurs, began to dominate. The earliest, most primitive reptiles, called anapsids, had one feature in common—the skull was a heavy box of bone with no openings other than for the eyes and nostrils. Because the jaw muscles were inside the skull, they were not very big and this meant that the mouth could not be opened very wide. Later reptiles, or diapsids, had a pair of openings, called fenestrae, either side of the skull behind the eye. The jaw muscles stretched across these holes, allowing the jaws to be opened wider.

Longisquama

A curious, lizardlike creature, *Longisquama* had a row of tall V-shaped scales rising from its back. Some experts believe that when these were held out at the animal's sides, they might have allowed it to glide short distances through the air, like gliding lizards today.

(P) Late Permian

Size: 24 in. (60 cm) long
Order: Millerosauria
Family: Millerettidae
Range: Africa: South Africa
Pn: MILL-er-ETT-ah

(T) Early Triassic

Size: 6 in. (15 cm) long
Order: Prolacertiformes
Family: Longisquamidae
Range: Asia
Pn: LONG-ih-SQUAM-a

Milleretta

Longisquama

Hylonomus

The remains of *Hylonomus*, one of the earliest reptiles known, have been found in the fossilized trunks of club moss trees. Floods buried the lower part of the trunks in mud, causing the trees to die and their interiors to rot away. Insects that gathered inside the trunks attracted *Hylonomus*. Once inside, the reptiles were unable to escape and were eventually fossilized.

(Ca) Middle Carboniferous

Size: 8 in. (20 cm) long
Order: Captorhinida
Family: Protorothyrididae
Range: North America: Nova Scotia
Pn: HY-lo-NOME-us

Milleretta

This small lizardlike creature was fast-moving and probably fed on insects. So far millerettids have only been found from the Late Permian period in South Africa. Although its skull did have openings on either side, *Milleretta* was a primitive anapsid reptile.

Hylonomus

Pareiasaurus

The largest of the early reptiles, pareiasaurs grew to lengths of up to 10 ft. (3 m). *Pareiasaurus* was typical, with its heavy body and back protected by plates of bone set into the skin. A plant eater, it had small teeth with serrated edges for chopping tough leaves.

(P) Middle
Permian

Size: 8 ft. (2.5 m) long
Order: Pareiasauria
Family: Pareiasauridae
Range: Africa; eastern Europe
Pn: par-EYE-ah-SAW-rus

Petrolacosaurus

One of the first diapsid reptiles, *Petrolacosaurus* had a slender lizardlike body. It had longer legs than a typical lizard and its tail was as long as its head and body combined. It probably chased insects to eat, snapping them up in its small sharp teeth.

Petrolacosaurus

(Ca) Late
Carboniferous

Size: 16 in. (40 cm) long
Order: Araeoscelidia
Family: Petrolacosauridae
Range: North America: Kansas
Pn: PET-rol-AK-oh-SAW-rus

Askeptosaurus

Askeptosaurus belonged to a family of diapsid reptiles known as thalattosaurs, which were adapted for life in the sea. It had a slender body, an extremely long tail and broad webbed feet. The long jaws were lined with many sharp teeth, ideal for catching fish.

Askeptosaurus

(T) Triassic

Size: 16 in. (40 cm) long
Order: Thalattosauria
Family: Askeptosauridae
Range: Europe: Switzerland
Pn: a-SKEPT-o-SAW-rus

Hypsognathus

Among the earliest reptiles were the procolophonids, which lived until the Late Triassic. *Hypsognathus* was one of the later members of the family. It had a wide squat body and was probably not a fast runner. The spikes around its head would have helped protect it from any enemies.

(T) Late
Triassic

Size: 13 in. (33 cm) long
Order: Procolophonia
Family: Procolophonidae
Range: North America: New Jersey
Pn: HIP-sog-NAY-thus

Hypsognathus

15

Carboniferous Times

The Carboniferous period began 354 million years ago and lasted until 290 million years ago. At the beginning of this time, the climate was warm and wet, but later it became cooler and more seasonal, and polar ice caps formed. During the Carboniferous, the first large forests grew, containing ginkgos, yew, and conifers. Tall clubmosses and horsetails also flourished. The first flying insects, such as giant dragonflies, filled the air. On land the first reptiles developed. They had a great advantage over amphibians—they could lay shelled eggs that were able to develop out of the water.

Coal swamps

This Carboniferous scene in what is now Nova Scotia shows life around a riverside swamp. At that time the climate there was much warmer than it is now. Plants include horsetails and giant clubmosses, and there are huge stumps and trunks of larger plants—ideal shelters for early reptiles such as *Hylonomus*. Most early reptiles were only about 8 in. (20 cm) long and looked much like modern lizards. They feasted on the giant insects of the time, biting through their tough outer skeletons with their sharp teeth.

Hylonomus

Troodon

Hylonomus

The Carboniferous world

During this time, the southern continents that made up the great land mass of Gondwana moved clockwise. This took its eastern part (India, Australia, and Antarctica) south and its western part (South America and Africa) north. A new ocean, the Tethys, opened in the east.

PACIFIC OCEAN

EQUATOR

TETHYS OCEAN

LAURENTIA

GONDWANA

Key to map

Ocean

Landmass

Sea-covered continent

Coal

Carboniferous means "coal-bearing." The plant debris from huge swamp forests (below) formed the world's first coal deposits, which in some places were hundreds of feet thick.

Mammal-like Reptiles

The first of these reptiles lived some 300 million years ago and dominated the Earth until the appearance of the dinosaurs in the Triassic. Pelycosaurs, the earliest group, lived in the Late Carboniferous and Early Permian. They rapidly evolved from small lizardlike creatures into animals of a heavier build with strong jaws and teeth of different shapes. Later, during the Permian, came several more advanced groups, such as the plant-eating dicynodonts, the carnivorous gorgonopsians, and the cynodonts. The cynodonts were the most advanced mammal-like reptiles and survived the longest. Among them were the direct ancestors of mammals, the dominant land animals today.

T Early
Triassic

Size: 3¼ ft. (1 m) long
Suborder: Cynodontia
Family: Cynognathidae
Range: Africa: South Africa; South America: Argentina
Pn: SIGH-nog-NAY-thus

Cynognathus

Cynognathus

One of the largest cynodonts, *Cynognathus* had a powerful body and a head that was more than 12 in. (30 cm) long. Its strong jaws show that it was a fierce hunter. Like mammals, it had three types of teeth: cutting incisor teeth, stabbing canines, and larger cheek teeth for chewing.

Edaphosaurus

P Early
Permian

Size: 10 ft. (3 m) long
Order: Pelycosauria
Family: Edaphosauridae
Range: Europe; North America: Texas
Pn: ee-daph-o-SAW-rus

Edaphosaurus

On its back, *Edaphosaurus* had long spines, which were probably covered with skin rich in blood vessels. This sail-like structure may have helped to control its temperature. The pelycosaur might have turned toward the sun to warm the blood as it flowed through the skin on the sail, and away from the sun and into the wind to cool down.

Kannemeyeria

A plant-eating reptile with a huge head, *Kannemeyeria* was one of the biggest of the dicynodonts. Strong heavy limbs supported the bulky body. It could have used its hard beak to tear up mouthfuls of leaves and roots, which it then ground down in its toothless jaws.

T Middle
Triassic

Size: 10 ft. (3 m) long
Suborder: Dicynodontia
Family: Kannemeyeriidae
Range: Africa: South Africa; Asia: India; South America: Argentina
Pn: KAN-eh-MAY-er-ee-a

Kannemeyeria

18

Oligokyphus

Lycaenops

This small, lightly built hunter had long, slender legs, and was probably a fast runner. It had strong jaws and large canine teeth, similar to those of the much later saber-toothed tigers. *Lycaenops* may have hunted in packs and preyed on large plant eaters such as *Moschops*.

J Early Jurassic

Size: 20 in. (50 cm) long
Suborder: Cynodontia
Family: Tritylodontidae
Range: Europe: England
Pn: OL-ig-oh-KY-fus

Oligokyphus

The tritylodonts, such as *Oligokyphus*, were the only mammal-like reptiles to survive into the Jurassic. A long-bodied, weasel-like creature, *Oligokyphus* was a plant eater. It had rows of highly specialized cheek teeth with sharp points that met as the jaws closed to give a precision bite.

Lycaenops

P Late Permian

Size: 3¼ ft. (1 m) long
Suborder: Gorgonopsia
Family: Gorgonopsidae
Range: Africa: South Africa
Pn: ly-KINE-ops

Lystrosaurus

Lystrosaurus had a short but very deep skull and stronger jaw muscles than most dicynodonts. The wide distribution of the fossils found is evidence that India and the southern continents were joined as one landmass in the Late Permian and Triassic.

T Early Triassic

Size: 3¼ ft. (1 m) long
Suborder: Dicynodontia
Family: Lystrosauridae
Range: Africa: South Africa; Asia: China; India; Antarctica; Europe
Pn: LISS-tro-SAW-rus

Moschops

This large plant-eating reptile had a massive skull and deep body. The bones of the forehead were up to 4 in. (10 cm) thick, suggesting that, like the bonehead dinosaurs (see pages 92–93), it might have taken part in headbutting battles with rivals in the herd.

Lystrosaurus

P Late Permian

Size: 16 ft. (5 m) long
Order: Therapsida
Family: Tapinocephalidae
Range: Africa: South Africa
Pn: MOS-chops

Moschops

Mammal-like Reptiles

The structure of the skull was an important feature of the more advanced mammal-like reptiles. It allowed for powerful muscles that made their jaws much stronger than those of other reptiles. The plant-eating dicynodonts, such as *Lystrosaurus*, *Robertia*, and *Dicynodon*, all had two downward-pointing tusks and a hard beak at the front of the jaws. Like mammals, carnivorous cynodonts, such as *Procynosuchus*, had different types of teeth for killing prey and chewing flesh.

Massetognathus

Despite its fierce appearance, *Massetognathus* was a plant eater and had large, broad teeth for crushing tough leaves. *Massetognathus* lived in South America during the Triassic period and was about 19 in. (48 cm) long.

Permian South Africa

In this Permian scene in what is now South Africa, there is a wide range of mammal-like reptiles. Plant eaters browse peacefully near the water's edge, but are watched by a hungry carnivore—*Lycaenops*. Another carnivore, *Procynosuchus*, lurks in the water. Amphibians such as *Peltobatrachus* feed alongside the reptiles. This creature's body was encased in bony armor to help protect it against carnivorous mammal-like reptiles.

Lycaenops

Lystrosaurus

Robertia

Peltobatrachus

Dimetrodon

This mammal-like reptile had a huge saillike structure on its back. The sail was made up of long spines extending up from the backbone. A sheet of skin, rich in blood vessels, covered the spines. The sail may have helped *Dimetrodon* control its body temperature. It could have turned the sail toward the sun to warm itself up and away from the sun and into a cooling breeze to cool down. *Dimetrodon* lived in North America during the Permian period and was about 10 ft. (3 m) long.

Much of the land that is now South Africa would have been dry and desertlike in Permian times. Plant life included horsetails, ferns, seed-ferns, and the first cycads and ginkgos.

Dicynodon

Lycaenops

Procynosuchus

Fern

21

Triassic Times

When the Triassic period began about 250 million years ago, life on the Earth was dominated by mammal-like reptiles, as well by other reptiles such as crocodiles. Frogs, turtles, and fish swam in rivers, and in the seas were marine reptiles such as ichthyosaurs and nothosaurs. Toward the end of the Triassic the first dinosaurs appeared and quickly spread across Pangaea. Many of the earlier reptiles had died out by the time the dinosaurs became the dominant large animals.

Triassic Germany

This scene in what is now southern Germany shows a group of plant-eating dinosaurs browsing on conifer branches. They are disturbed by the arrival of a predatory ceratosaur *Liliensternus*. Small crocodiles, *Terrestrisuchus*, and shrewlike mammals feed on insects in the tangled undergrowth of cycads and horsetails, while pterosaurs soar overhead.

Eudimorphodon, a flying reptile (pterosaur)

Liliensternus, a ceratosaur

Terrestrisuchus, a crocodile

Dragonfly

Fern

The Triassic world

In the Triassic period, the continents were all joined into one supercontinent, known as Pangaea, which lay across the Equator. This meant that the animals and plants of the time were able to spread across the world with ease. The climate was generally warm, with little variation, and there were no polar ice caps.

Asia

Europe

Germany

China

Central Asia

PANTHALASSIC OCEAN

North America

PALEO-TETHYS OCEAN

EQUATOR

PANGAEA

Africa

TETHYS OCEAN

India

Australia

Antarctica

Key to map

Ocean

Landmass

Sea-covered continent

Plateosaurus, a prosauropod

Peteinosaurus, a flying reptile (pterosaur)

Conifers

Thecodontosaurus, a prosauropod

Cycad

Moss

Shrewlike mammal

Triassic North America

In Triassic North America, there was much more desert than there is today. Most plants grew around lakes or the temporary pools that formed after heavy rainfall. This scene shows a variety of animals by a drying lake, including *Coelophysis*, a fast-moving predatory dinosaur, *Metoposaurus*, a giant amphibian, and *Trilphosaurus*, a plant-eating reptile. In the background is *Massospondylus*, one of the earliest long-necked dinosaurs.

Trilophosaurus

Metoposaurus

Massospondylus

Coelophysis

Turtles, Tortoises, and Terrapins

Proganochelys

Turtles and their relatives first appeared in the Late Triassic more than 200 million years ago. Even then, a typical turtle had a hard shell enclosing its body and probably looked remarkably like the turtles and tortoises of today. Like them, many of the prehistoric turtles could pull their head and legs into the shell for protection from enemies. The shell covering the back was made of bony plates, covered with a layer of smooth horn. Bony plates protected the underside. Like turtles and tortoises today, most early forms of turtles and tortoises had toothless jaws and a hard beak made of horn for cropping plants.

T Late Triassic

Size: 3¼ ft. (1 m) long
Order: Testudines
Family: Proganochelyidae
Range: Europe: Germany
Pn: PRO-gan-oh-KEEL-is

Proganochelys

This is one of the earliest turtles known. It had a broad, domed shell covering its back and bony plates protected its soft underside. It also had a number of extra plates around the edges of its shell, which gave the legs some protection. *Proganochelys* did have some teeth in its mouth, but it also had a toothless, horn-covered beak, like that of today's turtles.

Archelon

Archelon

This giant turtle did not have the heavy shell typical of most of its land and freshwater relatives. Instead, its body was protected by a framework of bony struts, which were probably covered by a thick layer of rubbery skin. Its limbs were massive paddles that it used to propel itself through water. Like modern leatherback turtles, *Archelon* may have fed on jellyfish.

Cr Late Cretaceous

Size: 12 ft. (3.7 m) long
Order: Testudines
Family: Protostegidae
Range: North America: Kansas, South Dakota
Pn: ar-KEE-lon

26

Meiolania

This large turtle had large bony spikes on its head. Two of these stuck out on either side, giving the head a width of about 24 in. (60 cm), and would have made it impossible for *Meiolania* to withdraw its head into its shell. The tail was encased in bony armor and ended in a spiked club.

Meiolania

Ple Pleistocene

Size: 8 ft. (2.5 m) long
Order: Testudines
Family: Meiolaniidae
Range: Australia
Pn: MY-oh-LAN-ee-ah

Pa Paleocene

Size: 18 in. (45 cm) long
Order: Testudines
Family: Trionychidae
Range: North America
Pn: PAY-lee-oh-TRY-on-ix

Paleotrionyx

Paleotrionyx was a soft-shelled turtle. Its low, rounded shell did not have a covering of horn protecting the bony plates. Instead, a layer of leathery skin covered the shell. It had a long mobile neck and a sharp beak, probably used to crop aquatic weeds and snap up insects and even small fish to eat.

Paleotrionyx

Stupendemys

The largest freshwater turtle ever, *Stupendemys* has been extinct for about 3 million years. (The largest freshwater turtle today is only 29 in. (75 cm) long. This giant lived in water, where it probably fed on weeds, like aquatic turtles today.

Pli Early Pliocene

Size: 6½ ft. (2 m) long
Order: Testudines
Family: Pelomedusidae
Range: South America: Venezuela
Pn: styoop-END-em-eez

Stupendemys

Testudo atlas

This was the largest land tortoise ever known and may have weighed as much as 4 tons. It was more than twice the length of the giant tortoises of today. *Testudo* probably fed on plants. If attacked, it would have pulled its head and legs into its heavy, bony shell for protection.

Ple Pleistocene

Size: 8 ft. (2.5 m) long
Order: Testudines
Family: Testudinidae
Range: Asia: India
Pn: TEST-oo-doh-AT-las

Testudo atlas

Lizards and Snakes

Today, lizards and snakes are a highly successful group of reptiles, with more than 7,000 species living all over the world except in Antarctica. The first known lizards were small, insect-eating creatures that lived in England during the mid Jurassic. By the Late Jurassic many different types of lizard had developed. Earlier groups of lizardlike reptiles include the sphenodonts, such as *Planocephalosaurus*, and aquatic reptiles such as *Hovasaurus*. Snakes may have evolved from long-bodied, water-living reptiles, such as *Pachyrhachis*.

Megalania

Ple Pleistocene

Size: 26 ft. (8 m) long
Order: Squamata
Family: Varanidae
Range: Australia
Pn: MEG-ah-LAN-ee-ah

Planocephalosaurus

The sphenodont group, to which this lizardlike creature belonged, first appeared in the Late Triassic. Today the only remaining sphenodont is the tuatara, found in New Zealand. A "living fossil," the tuatara has remained unchanged for 220 million years.

T Late Triassic

Size: 8 in. (20 cm) long
Order: Sphenodontida
Family: Sphenodontidae
Range: Europe: England
Pn: PLAN-oh-KEF-al-oh-SAW-rus

Planocephalosaurus

Plotosaurus

Mosasaurs such as *Plotosaurus* were sea-living lizards. The limbs were adapted into short flippers and at the end of the long tail was a vertical fin. The fin would have helped this marine lizard move its large body through the water.

Ardeosaurus

J Late Jurassic

Size: 5½ in. (14 cm) long
Order: Squamata
Family: Ardeosauridae
Range: Europe: Germany
Pn: AR-dee-oh-SAW-rus

Ardeosaurus

An early type of gecko, *Ardeosaurus* had the flattened head and large eyes typical of its modern relatives. Like them, it may have hunted insects and spiders at night, snapping them up in powerful jaws. With its slender body, long tail, and legs sprawled out sideways, *Ardeosaurus* looked very like the lizards of today.

Plotosaurus

28

Hovasaurus

This lizardlike, aquatic reptile had a tail that was twice the length of its body. The tail, which was deep and flattened from side-to-side, made an excellent paddle. *Hovasaurus* probably swallowed stones to help it sink in the water when diving for prey.

(P) Late Permian

Size: 20 in. (50 cm) long
Order: Lepidosauromorpha
Family: Tangasauridae
Range: Africa: Madagascar
Pn: HOVE-a-SAW-rus

Hovasaurus

Megalania

Monitor lizards first appeared in the Late Cretaceous and have changed little since. *Megalania* may have weighed four times as much as the Komodo dragon—the largest lizard alive today. It probably hunted large marsupials on the plains of Australia where it lived.

Pleurosaurus

Pleurosaurus belonged to a group of slender, snakelike sphenodonts which lived in water. The limbs were tiny, probably of little use on land, and the long tail could have been used to move the reptile through water. Pleurosaurs had extremely long bodies and some species had as many as 57 vertebrae.

(J) Late Jurassic

Size: 24 in. (60 cm) long
Order: Sphenodontida
Family: Pleurosauridae
Range: Europe: Germany
Pn: PLOO-roh-SAW-rus

Pleurosaurus

Pachyrhachis

A water-living lizard, *Pachyrhachis* had the long body of a snake and the large head of a monitor lizard. It had tiny back legs and swam by snakelike movements of its long body. This reptile may be one of the ancestors of today's snakes.

(Cr) Early Cretaceous

Size: 3¼ ft. (1 m) long
Order: Squamata
Family: Pachyrhachidae
Range: Asia: Israel
Pn: PAK-ee-RAK-iss

(Cr) Late Cretaceous

Size: 33 ft. (10 m) long
Order: Squamata
Family: Mosasauridae
Range: North America: Kansas
Pn: PLOT-oh-SAW-rus

Pachyrhachis

Placodonts and Nothosaurs

During the time of the dinosaurs, there were several groups of marine reptiles. Least well adapted to marine life were the placodonts of the Triassic. These semiaquatic reptiles were equally at home on the shore or in shallow water, searching for shellfish to eat. Nothosaurs were better suited to life in the sea. They were fish eaters and typically had a streamlined body, long tail, and webbed feet. Both placodonts and nothosaurs died out at the end of the Triassic. Claudiosaurs were an earlier group of semiaquatic reptiles that lived in the Late Permian. They may have been a link between land-living reptiles and later marine reptiles such as nothosaurs and plesiosaurs.

(T) Triassic

Size: 13 ft. (4 m) long
Order: Nothosauria
Family: Nothosauridae
Range: Europe
Pn: seh-REEZ-ee-oh-SAW-rus

Ceresiosaurus

This nothosaur swam by moving its long body and tail from side to side. Like the plesiosaurs of the Jurassic, it used two pairs of paddlelike flippers rather than limbs to help move itself through water. The front flippers were larger than the back flippers and may have provided most of the steering and braking power.

Pistosaurus

Pistosaurus

This marine reptile had features of both the nothosaurs and the plesiosaurs (see pages 32–33). Its body is similar to that of other nothosaurs, but it had a stiff backbone like the plesiosaurs. This meant that it used its paddlelike limbs to push itself through water rather than moving its body and tail.

(T) Triassic

Size: 10 ft. (3 m) long
Order: Nothosauria
Family: Pistosauridae
Range: Europe: France, Germany
Pn: PISS-toe-SAW-rus

Nothosaurus

This typical nothosaur probably lived much as seals do today—fishing at sea and resting on land. Its body and tail were long and flexible and the long toes on each foot were probably webbed for swimming. Its long, slim jaws were lined with sharp teeth—ideal for catching fish.

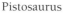
Nothosaurus

(T) Triassic

Size: 10 ft. (3 m) long
Order: Nothosauria
Family: Nothosauridae
Range: Asia: China, Israel, Russia; Europe; North Africa
Pn: NOTHE-oh-SAW-rus

Ceresiosaurus

(T) Middle
Triassic

Size: 24 in. (60 cm) long
Order: Nothosauria
Family: Nothosauridae
Range: Europe: Spain
Pn: LAH-ree-oh-SAW-rus

Lariosaurus

One of the smaller
nothosaurs,
Lariosaurus probably
spent much of its time
walking on the shore and
paddling in shallow coastal water,
feeding on small fish and shrimp.
It had a shorter neck than most
nothosaurs and small toes that
would not have been much use
for swimming.

Lariosaurus

(T) Late
Triassic

Size: 3¼ ft. (1 m) long
Order: Placodontia
Family: Henodontidae
Range: Europe: Germany
Pn: HEN-oh-dus

Henodus

Henodus

This placodont had a square-
shaped body, covered with bony
plates. These made a strong shell
to protect it from attack by
other marine reptiles such as
ichthyosaurs. Although toothless,
Henodus probably had a horn-
covered beak like that of a turtle,
which it could use to crush prey
such as shellfish.

Claudiosaurus

This lizardlike creature probably
lived much like modern marine
iguanas. Like them, it may have
spent a good deal of its time
resting on rocky beaches,
warming its body before going
hunting. In water, it held its legs
against its body to give a more
streamlined shape as it searched
for food among seaweeds and
rocks.

(P) Late
Permian

Size: 24 in. (60 cm) long
Order: Lepidosauromorpha
Family: Claudiosauridae
Range: Africa: Madagascar
Pn: CLAWED-ee-oh-SAW-rus

Claudiosaurus

(T) Early to
Middle Triassic

Size: 6½ ft. (2 m) long
Order: Placodontia
Family: Placodontidae
Range: Europe: Alps
Pn: PLAK-oh-dus

Placodus

Placodus had a stocky body
and its only aquatic features
were its webbed feet and long
tail. Its teeth suggest that it
fed mostly on shellfish.
Placodus could have plucked
shellfish from the rocks with
the blunt teeth sticking out at
the front of its jaws and then
crushed them with the broad,
flat back teeth.

Placodus

31

Plesiosaurs and Ichthyosaurs

Plesiosaurs and ichthyosaurs were the most successful of all the marine reptiles. They dominated the world's seas throughout the Jurassic and Cretaceous periods. There were two groups of plesiosaurs—pliosaurs and the plesiosaurs themselves. Plesiosaurs had long necks and short heads and fed on smaller sea creatures. Pliosaurs were fierce hunters. With their powerful jaws, they could catch sharks and large squid. The ichthyosaurs were best adapted of all to marine life. Typically, they had a streamlined, fishlike body, and a tail that could beat from side-to-side to power their high-speed swimming.

Ophthalmosaurus

(J) Late Jurassic

Size: 11½ ft. (3.5 m) long
Order: Ichthyosauria
Family: Ichthyosauridae
Range: Europe: England, France; western North America; South America: Argentina
Pn: OFF-thal-moh-SAW-rus

Ophthalmosaurus

This ichthyosaur had huge eyes, measuring up to 4 in. (10 cm) across. A ring of bony plates surrounded each eyeball to keep the soft eye from collapsing under the pressure of the water. The large eyes of the *Ophthalmosaurus* suggest that it probably hunted at night.

Elasmosaurus

Elasmosaurus was the longest known plesiosaur. Its neck measured 26 ft. (8 m)—more than half of its total length—and contained as many as 71 vertebrae. Its head was relatively small and its jaws were lined with sharply pointed teeth. It probably fed on fish, plunging its long neck into the water to seize its prey.

Elasmosaurus

(Cr) Late Cretaceous

Size: 46 ft. (14 m) long
Order: Plesiosauria
Family: Elasmosauridae
Range: Asia: Japan; North America: Kansas
Pn: eh-LAZ-mo-SAW-rus

Shonisaurus

Liopleurodon

A heavily built pliosaur, *Liopleurodon* had a large head, short, thick neck, and a streamlined body. It had big, powerful flippers and would have been able to swim long distances as it chased fast-moving prey such as squid and even other plesiosaurs and ichthyosaurs.

Plesiosaurus

J Early Jurassic

Size: 7½ ft. (2.3 m) long
Order: Plesiosauria
Family: Plesiosauridae
Range: Europe: England, Germany
Pn: PLEEZ-ee-oh-SAW-rus

Liopleurodon

J Late Jurassic

Size: 39 ft. (12 m) long
Order: Plesiosauria
Family: Pliosauridae
Range: Asia: Russia; Europe: England, France, Germany
Pn: LY-oh-PLOO-ro-don

J Early Jurassic **Cr** Early Cretaceous

Size: 6½ ft. (2 m) long
Order: Ichthyosauria
Family: Ichthyosauridae
Range: Europe: England, Germany; Greenland; North America: Alberta
Pn: IK-thee-oh-SAW-rus

Plesiosaurus

A typical plesiosaur, with its long neck and small head, *Plesiosaurus* fed on small squid and fish. Its long neck meant that it could have raised its head high above the surface of the sea to search for signs of prey. If it spotted something, it could make a swift lunge to seize the animal in its mouth.

Ichthyosaurus

Ichthyosaurus

So many fossils of *Ichthyosaurus* have been found that it is one of the best known of all prehistoric animals. In some of these fossils, the tiny bones of young were inside the adult bodies, showing that ichthyosaurs, like dolphins today, gave birth to live young at sea.

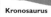

T Late Triassic

Size: 49 ft. (15 m) long
Order: Ichthyosauria
Family: Shastasauridae
Range: North America: Nevada
Pn: SHOWN-ih-SAW-rus

Kronosaurus

Shonisaurus

The biggest of the ichthyosaurs, *Shonisaurus* had extremely long jaws, with teeth only at the front. All of its paddlelike flippers were about the same length—in most ichthyosaurs the front flippers were longer than the back pair.

Kronosaurus

The largest-known pliosaur, *Kronosaurus* had a huge, flat-topped skull, measuring almost a quarter of its total body length. A fierce predator, it moved at high speed, flapping its strong flippers up and down as though flying through the water.

Cr Early Cretaceous

Size: 42 ft. (12.8 m) long
Order: Plesiosauria
Family: Pliosauridae
Range: Australia: Queensland
Pn: KRONE-oh-SAW-rus

33

Sea Creatures

In the time of the dinosaurs the seas were packed with life. Fish such as *Lepidotes*, their bodies protected by thick bony scales, hunted worms, mollusks, and other small creatures. Crinoids, animals related to starfish, lived on the seabed, catching tiny prey in their feathery, many-branched arms. Also common were belemnites and ammonites, extinct relatives of octopus and squid. Ammonites had a soft body coiled inside a shell with many chambers, whereas belemnites had a straight body and long tentacles, similar to today's squid. Among the biggest creatures were the many types of marine reptiles, such as ichthyosaurs and plesiosaurs, which cruised the oceans preying on fish, squid, and belemnites.

Underwater birth

Ichthyosaurs are thought to have given birth underwater. The young came out tail first, like those of dolphins and whales. This fossil shows a female ichthyosaur with her young just emerging from her body.

In this **Jurassic ocean**, a school of belemnites scatters as an *Ichthyosaurus* swims into them, grasping prey in its long jaws. Meanwhile another ichthyosaur, *Eurhinosaurus*, rises to the surface to take a breath.

Ammonite

Plesiosaurus

Lepidotes

Long slender snout

Dimorphodon

Bones supporting tail

Paddlelike front limb

SKELETON OF AN ICHTHYOSAUR

Marine reptiles

A typical ichthyosaur had a streamlined body, similar to that of a dolphin today. The main swimming power was provided by the large tail, which beat to and fro as the reptile sped through the water. The paddlelike front limbs were used for steering.

Eurhinosaurus

Ichthyosaurus

Belemnite

35

Crinoid

Beast of Maastricht

In 1786 the amazing discovery of some huge jaw bones was made in a quarry near Maastricht in Holland. Years later, scientists realized that the bones belonged to a type of giant water-dwelling lizard that lived during the Late Cretaceous—a mosasaur. At that time, water would have covered the area and would have been home to a wide range of marine animals. Some 350 years later in 1998, scientists working in the same quarry made another important find—a nearly complete skeleton of a mosasaur measuring about 46 ft. (14 m) long. Mosasaur remains have also been found in other parts of Europe, North America, Africa, Australia, and New Zealand.

Mosasaurs

These giant marine lizards lived in all oceans in the Late Cretaceous, but became extinct at the end of the period 65 million years ago. There may have been as many as 70 species. The smallest of these, *Carinodens*, was about 10 ft. (3 m) long and may have lived on the sea floor, preying on mollusks and sea urchins. The largest was *Mosasaurus hoffmani* which grew to 50 ft. (15 m) long. Mosasaurs were fast swimmers, pushing themselves through the water by moving their huge tails from side to side. The paddlelike flippers were used to help steer the body.

Tail moved from side to side for swimming power

36

Ocean predator

Mosasaurus hoffmani had a powerful skull and long jaws lined with strong teeth able to bite and crush prey. It probably snapped up fish and squid, but may also have attacked ammonites—shelled relatives of squid. Many ammonite shells have been found showing marks made by teeth shaped like those of mosasaurs. Some of these shells appear to have been bitten several times from different angles as the mosasaur struggled to reach the flesh inside.

Huge, powerful jaws

Mosasaurus hoffmani

Flippers

Sensational find

The engraving below shows the discovery of the massive jaw bones of *Mosasaurus hoffmani*. The bones were found in an old chalk mine in Maastricht, Holland, in 1786 and caused enormous excitement among European scientists. Experts disagreed as to what the creature might be. Dutch naturalist Pieter Camper decided it was a whale, but later his son realized it was a huge lizard. French paleontologist Baron Georges Cuvier named the creature *Mosasaurus*, meaning "lizard from the River Meuse."

Plesiosaurs

Plesiosaurs were well adapted for life in water and spent nearly all their time at sea. But, like turtles today, they did have to come on to the land to lay eggs. The females dragged themselves on to the shore and laid their eggs in pits they had dug in the sand. When the young plesiosaurs hatched, they made their own way down to the sea. Most plesiosaurs had long slender necks, but there was one group of short-necked plesiosaurs, called pliosaurs.

Swimming and feeding

A plesiosaur's long, narrow flippers were similar in shape to those of penguins and turtles today. As the plesiosaur swam, it beat these flippers up and down in slow steady movements as though "flying" through the water (below). To feed, the plesiosaur opened its mouth wide to take in small fish and shrimp as well as water. When it closed its jaws, the teeth acted like a strainer so water could flow out, leaving any food inside the mouth to be swallowed.

Underwater battle

This Jurassic underwater scene shows long-necked plesiosaurs (*Plesiosaurus*) and a short-necked pliosaur (*Rhomaleosaurus*) swimming among ammonites and fish. The pliosaurs were fierce predators with large heads and strong jaws, and could swim faster than their plesiosaur relatives. The long slender neck of *Plesiosaurus* made it an easy target for predators.

Ammonite

Rhomaleosaurus

Inside a plesiosaur

This skeleton belonged to a long-necked plesiosaur named *Cryptoclidus*. The skull is small compared to the body, and the jaws are lined with sharp teeth. Large shoulder bones and hip bones supported powerful muscles for moving the long flippers. Each toe in the flippers contained as many as ten bones, which made them very flexible. Belly ribs made the plesiosaur's body strong and helped to support the movements of the flippers.

Cryptoclidus was a plesiosaur that lived in European seas during the late Jurassic period. It grew to about 13 ft. (4 m) long.

Plesiosaurus

Plesiosaurus

Coelacanth

39

Early Ruling Reptiles

Rutiodon

Archosaurs, or ruling reptiles, were the group to which dinosaurs belonged. There were several different groups of archosaurs, but the only ones that survive today are the crocodiles. Among the earliest were the proterosuchids, some of which were hunters that resembled crocodiles. Others lived on land. Later came the crurotarsans, such as *Ornithosuchus*, and the aquatic phytosaurs. Aetosaurs, such as *Desmatosuchus*, were the first plant-eating archosaurs and they spread throughout much of the world.

> (T) Middle
> Triassic
> **Size:** 10 ft. (3 m) long
> **Order:** Crurotarsi
> **Family:** Phytosauridae
> **Range:** Europe: Germany, Switzerland; North America
> **Pn:** ROOT-ee-oh-don

> (T) Early
> Triassic
> **Size:** 6½ ft. (2 m) long
> **Order:** Archosauria
> **Family:** Proterosuchidae
> **Range:** Asia: China
> **Pn:** PROH-ter-oh-SOO-kus

Rutiodon

Phytosaurs, such as *Rutiodon*, lived in rivers and lakes, where they fed on fish and other creatures. The body was heavily armored with plates of bone. The long jaws were filled with sharp teeth. Phytosaurs looked very similar to modern crocodiles, but their nostrils were positioned on a bony bump near the eyes, not at the end of the snout as in crocodiles.

Proterosuchus

An early proterosuchid, this reptile looked much like a modern crocodile and probably lived in much the same way. It had a slender body and short legs, which sprawled out at the sides of the body. It may have hunted mammal-like reptiles on land as well as fish in water.

Proterosuchus

Erythrosuchus

This early archosaur was one of the biggest land predators of its time. It had a large head and strong jaws lined with sharp teeth. Its legs were held more directly under the body than those of the sprawling *Proterosuchus*, allowing it to move well on land.

Desmatosuchus

Despite its fierce appearance, *Desmatosuchus* was a plant eater with small, leaf-shaped teeth. The bulky body was encased in heavy plates of bone, and a pair of spines, up to 18 in. (45 cm) long, projected sideways from its shoulders. The body armor defended bulky, slow-moving *Desmatosuchus* from predators.

> (T) Early
> Triassic
> **Size:** 15 ft. (4.5 m) long
> **Order:** Archosauria
> **Family:** Erythrosuchidae
> **Range:** Africa: South Africa
> **Pn:** er-ITH-ro-SOOK-us

Erythrosuchus

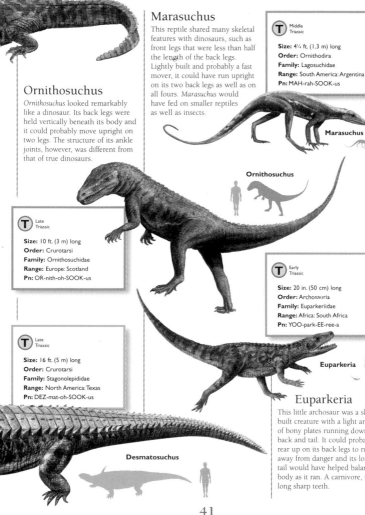

Marasuchus

This reptile shared many skeletal features with dinosaurs, such as front legs that were less than half the length of the back legs. Lightly built and probably a fast mover, it could have run upright on its two back legs as well as on all fours. *Marasuchus* would have fed on smaller reptiles as well as insects.

T Middle Triassic

Size: 4¼ ft. (1.3 m) long
Order: Ornithodira
Family: Lagosuchidae
Range: South America: Argentina
Pn: MAH-rah-SOOK-us

Marasuchus

Ornithosuchus

Ornithosuchus looked remarkably like a dinosaur. Its back legs were held vertically beneath its body and it could probably move upright on two legs. The structure of its ankle joints, however, was different from that of true dinosaurs.

Ornithosuchus

T Late Triassic

Size: 10 ft. (3 m) long
Order: Crurotarsi
Family: Ornithosuchidae
Range: Europe: Scotland
Pn: OR-nith-oh-SOOK-us

T Early Triassic

Size: 20 in. (50 cm) long
Order: Archosauria
Family: Euparkeriidae
Range: Africa: South Africa
Pn: YOO-park-EE-ree-a

Euparkeria

T Late Triassic

Size: 16 ft. (5 m) long
Order: Crurotarsi
Family: Stagonolepididae
Range: North America: Texas
Pn: DEZ-mat-oh-SOOK-us

Desmatosuchus

Euparkeria

This little archosaur was a slimly built creature with a light armor of bony plates running down its back and tail. It could probably rear up on its back legs to run away from danger and its long tail would have helped balance its body as it ran. A carnivore, it had long sharp teeth.

Crocodiles

The first crocodiles appeared in the Triassic, some 220 million years ago, and are the only members of the archosaur, or ruling reptile group (see pages 40–41), alive today. The earliest examples of the order Crocodylia, such as *Terrestrisuchus*, were lightly built long-legged creatures, which probably fed on insects. True crocodiles evolved in the Jurassic and look remarkably similar to modern crocodiles. Some lived on land, whereas others were semiaquatic as crocodiles are today. A few families, such as the metriorhynchs, were adapted to life in the sea. All crocodiles, even the early ones, have long narrow skulls with muscles set far back to allow the jaws to open wide for grasping large prey.

J Middle to Late Jurassic

Size: 10 ft. (3 m) long
Order: Crocodylia
Family: Metriorhynchidae
Range: Europe: England, France; South America: Chile
Pn: MET-ree-oh-RINK-us

Metriorhynchus

This crocodile and other members of its family were well adapted for life in the sea. Its limbs were paddlelike flippers and its tail had a large fishlike fin for swimming. It did not have bony protective plates on its body like crocodiles today—these would have made its body too heavy in the water.

Protosuchus

J Early Jurassic

Size: 3 ft. (90 cm) long
Order: Crocodylia
Family: Protosuchidae
Range: North America: Arizona
Pn: PROE-toh-SOOK-us

Protosuchus

Fossils of *Protosuchus* have been found in the same rocks as the remains of dinosaurs. This suggests that this land-living crocodile preyed on other land creatures. Like today's crocodiles, *Protosuchus* had a pair of long teeth at the front of the lower jaw that fitted into notches on the upper jaw when the mouth was closed.

Deinosuchus

Only a skull, measuring more than 6½ ft. (2 m), has been found of *Deinosuchus*, showing that it was probably the biggest crocodile of all time. It may have lived much like the crocodiles of today, but some scientists believe that *Deinosuchus* had longer legs than modern crocodiles and lived on land, preying on dinosaurs.

Cr Late Cretaceous

Size: 49 ft. (15 m) long
Order: Crocodylia
Family: Alligatoridae
Range: North America: Texas
Pn: DINE-oh-SOOK-us

Terrestrisuchus

An early member of the crocodile group, this lightly built reptile had long back legs and may have moved upright. It probably fed on insects and other small creatures. Although *Terrestrisuchus* does not look like a crocodile, there are many typical features of the group in the bone structure of its skull and front limbs.

Metriorhynchus

Bernissartia

This little crocodile probably lived in water and on land. It had two types of teeth in its jaws. At the front were long, pointed teeth, suitable for catching fish. At the back were broader, flatter teeth, which could have been used to crush shellfish or the bones of dead animals.

T Late Triassic

Size: 20 in. (50 cm) long
Order: Crocodylia
Family: Saltoposuchidae
Range: Europe: Wales
Pn: ter-EST-ri-SOOK-us

Terrestrisuchus

Bernissartia

Cr Early Cretaceous

Size: 24 in. (60 cm) long
Order: Crocodylia
Family: Bernissartiidae
Range: Europe: Belgium, England
Pn: BER-nih-SART-ee-ah

Deinosuchus

Teleosaurus

A sea-living crocodile, *Teleosaurus* had extremely long, narrow jaws lined with many sharp teeth. These teeth interlocked when the mouth was closed, forming a trap ideal for catching slippery fish or squid. It probably swam by moving its long slender body and tail, with its short front legs held against its body.

Teleosaurus

J Early Jurassic

Size: 10 ft. (3 m) long
Order: Crocodylia
Family: Teleosauridae
Range: Europe: France
Pn: TELL-ee-oh-SAW-rus

43

Flying Reptiles

Pterosaurs were the first vertebrates (animals with backbones) to take to the air. They first evolved in the Late Triassic and became extinct at the end of the Cretaceous at the same time as the dinosaurs. More than 120 different species of pterosaur have been discovered so far. All had wings that were attached to an extremely long fourth finger on each hand and to the sides of the pterosaur's body. The earliest pterosaurs were the rhamphorhynchoids, which had a long tail and short neck. Later came the pterodactyloids, which grew much larger and typically had a short tail and long neck and skull.

J Late Jurassic

Size: 3¼ ft. (1 m) wingspan
Order: Pterosauria
Family: Rhamphorhynchidae
Range: Europe: Germany; Africa: Tanzania
Pn: RAM-for-INK-us

Rhamphorhynchus

Eudimorphodon

T Late Triassic

Size: 29 in. (75 cm) wingspan
Order: Pterosauria
Family: Dimorphodontidae
Range: Europe: Italy
Pn: yoo-dee-MORF-oh-don

Eudimorphodon

This rhamphorhynchoid is one of the earliest pterosaurs known. It had a long bony tail, which made up about half its total length. Like many other pterosaurs, it had a small diamond-shaped flap at the tip of the tail that may have acted like a rudder to help the pterosaur change direction in the air.

J Late Jurassic

Size: 3¼ ft. (1 m) wingspan
Order: Pterosauria
Family: Rhamphorhynchidae
Range: Europe: England
Pn: SKAF-og-NAY-thus

Scaphognathus

Studies of the brain cavity of one fossil of this pterosaur have shown that its brain was much larger than that of other reptiles of a similar size. The relative sizes of different areas of the brain suggest that this pterosaur, and probably its relatives, had excellent eyesight, but a poor sense of smell.

Scaphognathus

Quetzalcoatlus

Although known only from a few wing bones, this pterodactyloid is thought to have been the biggest flying animal ever. Its remains were found in an area of Texas that was once marshland. Like a giant egret, *Quetzalcoatlus* may have waded through the marsh, snatching fish with its long jaws.

Rhamphorhynchus

Well-preserved fossils of this pterosaur found in the limestone of Solnhofen in Germany reveal even the fine structure of its wings. These show that thin fibers ran from the front to the back of the wings, giving them extra strength. This pterosaur had long jaws filled with sharp teeth and probably fed on fish.

Dimorphodon

This pterosaur had an unusually large head, similar in shape to a puffin's. Inside the mouth were two types of teeth— spiky ones at the front and much smaller teeth farther back. These may have helped the pterosaur to catch insects in the air or on the ground.

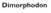

J Early Jurassic

Size: 29 in. (75 cm) wingspan
Order: Pterosauria
Family: Dimorphodontidae
Range: Europe: England
Pn: dy-MORF-oh-don

Dimorphodon

Pterodaustro

Pterodactylus

Like many pterosaurs, *Pterodactylus* probably fed on fish. Its long narrow jaws, lined with sharp teeth, would have been ideal for grasping and holding its slippery prey. With its short tail and long neck, it was a typical pterodactyloid.

Pterodactylus

J Late Jurassic

Size: 4 ft. (1.2 m) wingspan
Order: Pterosauria
Family: Pterodaustridae
Range: South America: Argentina
Pn: TER-oh-DOW-stro

Quetzalcoatlus

Cr Late Cretaceous

Size: 39 ft. (12 m) wingspan
Order: Pterosauria
Family: Azhdarchidae
Range: North America: Texas
Pn: KWET-zal-KO-at-lus

J Late Jurassic

Size: 29 in. (75 cm) wingspan
Order: Pterosauria
Family: Pterodactylidae
Range: Europe: England, France, Germany; Africa: Tanzania
Pn: TER-oh-DAK-ty-lus

Pterodaustro

Pterodaustro had long jaws, which curved upward at the tips. The lower jaw was packed with fine teeth, and there were also tiny teeth in the upper jaw. It may have fed by skimming along the surface of the sea. As water flowed through its open mouth, tiny creatures would have been caught on the sievelike teeth.

Dsungaripterus

This pterosaur had a small backward-pointing crest on the top of its head and a long bony crest on its snout. Its narrow jaws curved upward slightly at the tip. It may have fed on hard-shelled prey such as mollusks, which it crushed using its broad, flat teeth.

Dsungaripterus

Cr Early Cretaceous

Size: 10 ft. (3 m) wingspan
Order: Pterosauria
Family: Dsungaripteridae
Range: Asia: China
Pn: jung-gah-RIP-ter-us

Cr Late Cretaceous

Size: 23 ft. (7 m) wingspan
Order: Pterosauria
Family: Pteranodontidae
Range: Europe and North America
Pn: te-RAN-o-don

Pteranodon

Criorhynchus

J Late Jurassic

Size: 24 in. (60 cm) wingspan
Order: Pterosauria
Family: Rhamphorhynchidae
Range: Asia: Kazakhstan
Pn: SOR-dees

Cr Late Cretaceous

Size: 16.5 ft. (5 m) wingspan
Order: Pterosauria
Family: Criorhynchidae
Range: Europe: England
Pn: Kri-o-RING-kus

Sordes

Fossils of this flying reptile show that its body, but not its tail or wings, may have been covered with a thick coat of hair. The hair would have helped to keep the body warm. Some experts believe that this is proof that at least some pterosaurs may have been warmblooded like birds today.

Sordes

Criorhynchus

This pterosaur had a strange rounded tip to its long jaws. Like all pterosaurs, it would have moved on the ground as well as in the air. Some experts think that pterosaurs crawled along on all fours, using the claws on their wings as well as their feet. Others believe that they walked upright on their back legs like birds today.

Anurognathus

This little rhamphorhynchoid had a deep head and short jaws filled with strong peglike teeth. It may have fed on insects—its short tail and small body would have made it a fast, agile flier, able to pursue speedy flying insects.

J Late Jurassic

Size: 18 in. (50 cm) wingspan
Order: Pterosauria
Family: Anurognathidae
Range: Europe: Germany
Pn: a-noo-ROG-na-thus

Anurognathus

Pteranodon

Pteranodon was one of the longest winged of all pterosaurs. It had no teeth in its long jaws and may have fed like a pelican today, simply scooping up fish and swallowing them whole. The large backward-pointing crest on its head may have used in courtship displays—females would have been attracted to the males with the largest crests.

Cearadactylus

The jaws of this pterosaur spread out slightly at the tip into a spoon shape, and several large teeth stuck out around the edges. When the mouth was closed, the teeth formed a trap, ideal for catching slippery fish. This pterosaur is known only from a single incomplete fossil skull.

Cearadactylus

Cr Early Cretaceous

Size: 13 ft. (4 m) wingspan
Order: Pterosauria
Family: Cearadactylidae
Range: South America: Brazil
Pn: say-ahr-ah-DAK-ti-lus

Nyctosaurus

Cr Late Cretaceous

Size: 9½ ft. (2.9 m) wingspan
Order: Pterosauria
Family: Nyctosauridae
Range: North America, South America: Brazil
Pn: nik-to-SORE-us

Nyctosaurus

Like *Pteranodon*, *Nyctosaurus* had long, sharp, toothless jaws. It, too, probably fed on fish which it swallowed whole. It had a huge wingspan and could have glided long distances over the oceans, searching for prey.

Flying Reptiles

Pterosaurs lived at the same time as dinosaurs and may share the same ancestor. Scientists now believe that these flying reptiles were good, if slow, fliers, able to flap their wings as birds do, rather than just gliding through the air. They may not have been able to take off from the ground but could have launched themselves into the air from a perch in a tree or on a rock. Pterosaurs ate a range of foods. Those with long skulls and sharp teeth probably fed on fish. Others may have caught insects or even fed on plants. The long beak of *Tapejara*, for example, may have been used to pick fruit.

Cearadactylus

This pterosaur, named **Pterodactylus,** lived in Europe in Jurassic times. The well-preserved fossil clearly shows the body structure, including the slender jaws and the extra-long fingers that supported the wings.

Pterosaur skeleton

A pterosaur had an extremely light skeleton so that it was able to fly. Its bones were slender and many were also hollow to make them lighter still. Its first three fingers were short and tipped with sharp claws, but the fourth finger was very long and helped to support the wing. The wing was also attached to the side of the body. On each foot were five toes. Four were long and tipped with claws. The fifth toe was short and did not have a claw.

Shoulder bone

Skull

Short tail

Long fourth finger

Santanadactylus

Cretaceous pterosaurs

In this scene of 100 million years ago, pterosaurs soar over the ocean, searching for fish to catch. *Tapejara*, a pterosaur with a huge prow on its upper jaw, heads inland. On the rocks *Tropeognathus* moves around on all fours, using the claws on its wings as well as its feet.

Tropeognathus

Tapejara

A Late Cretaceous pterosaur, *Anhanguera* probably fed on fish, swooping down to the surface of the sea to grasp its prey and carrying it off to eat. Its long slender jaws and sharp teeth were ideally shaped for holding slippery fish.

Flying Reptiles in the Early Cretaceous

In this Early Cretaceous scene on the landmass now known as Asia, two huge *Dsungaripterus* pterosaurs swoop down to a river to find food. *Dsungaripterus* had a wingspan of as much as 10 ft. (3 m) and long narrow jaws that curved up at the tip. These jaws could have been used like pliers to prize shellfish from crevices or rocks. This pterosaur had a long bony crest on the top of its head. Plants such as cycads, conifers, and horsetails grow around the lake. A variety of dinosaurs are feasting on the plant life, including *Iguanodon*, *Probactrosaurus*, and long-necked *Euhelopus*.

Euhelopus

Dsungaripterus

Probactrosaurus

Horsetails

Iguanodon

Cycad

Conifer
tree

Dinosaurs

These amazing reptiles were probably the most successful animals that have ever lived. The first dinosaurs lived about 225 million years ago, during the Triassic period, and more and more species developed during the Jurassic and Cretaceous periods. Dinosaurs became large and widespread until they mysteriously disappeared at the end of the Cretaceous about 65 million years ago.

Dinosaurs were living, breathing creatures that had to find food, defend themselves against enemies, and look after their young—just as animals do today. Although no human has ever seen a living dinosaur, we know something of how they looked and the way they behaved from the fossils and other remains that have been discovered. Bones show the shape and size of dinosaurs, teeth provide clues about what they ate, while fossil tracks can give an idea of how fast they moved.

With its huge, daggerlike teeth and powerful jaws, *Allosaurus* would have been a fearsome sight as it preyed on plant-eating dinosaurs. It lived in Jurassic times and its fossilized remains have been found in western North America.

Corythosaurus

What was a dinosaur?

A dinosaur was a type of reptile that had a bony skeleton and thick leathery skin. More than 500 species of dinosaurs have been discovered so far, and there may be many more yet to be found. They ranged in size from creatures of 3¼ ft. (1 m) long to giants of 100 ft. (30 m) or more. Dinosaurs lived on land and are believed to have laid eggs. There were two groups of dinosaurs, saurischians and ornithischians, which differed in the structure of their hip bones. All ornithischians fed on plants, but the saurischian group included fierce, meat-eating hunters as well as plant eaters.

Lizard

Ways of moving

Most early reptiles moved like lizards today, with their legs sprawled out to the sides. Dinosaurs had a much better way of moving. Their legs were held straight down beneath the body, which meant they could carry more weight and take longer, faster strides.

Dinosaur

A **dramatic encounter** between the meat-eating tyrannosaur *Albertosaurus* and the plant-eating horned dinosaur *Centrosaurus* is reconstructed in this display at the Royal Tyrrell Museum in Drumheller, Canada.

A skeleton of the ornithischian dinosaur *Iguanodon*

The two groups of dinosaurs

Saurischian dinosaurs, such as *Ornitholestes*, had a pubis bone that pointed away from the ischium bone. In ornithischian dinosaurs, such as *Iguanodon*, the pubis bone ran below the ischium bone. Of the dinosaurs known, about 55 percent belong to the saurischian group and 45 percent to the ornithischian group. Saurischians included the sauropods, the biggest of all dinosaurs.

Ischium

Pubis

Ischium

Pubis

A skeleton of the saurischian dinosaur *Ornitholestes*

Dinosaur legs

Slender, birdlike dinosaurs, such as *Gallimimus*, had long thigh and calf bones with big muscles in the thigh to power the leg. The ankle and foot bones were also long and slim. Such dinosaurs could probably run up to 40 mph (65 km/h). The legs of sauropods such as *Camarasaurus* were very different. The bones were large and bulky and the foot spread out to form a large pad to support the dinosaur's massive weight. Sauropods plodded along on all four legs, whereas *Gallimimus* ran on its two slender back legs.

Thigh bone

Thigh bone

Calf bone

Leg of *Camarasaurus*

Back leg of *Gallimimus*

Calf bones

Long slender ankle bones

Short thick ankle bones

Slim three-toed foot

Heavy five-toed foot

A Dinosaur Family Tree

The word "dinosaur," meaning "terrible lizard," was first used in 1842 by Richard Owen, one of the first experts on these reptiles. Since then, views on the relationships between the different groups of dinosaurs have changed dramatically as more species are found and new discoveries made. The chart here shows a dinosaur family tree that is accepted by most experts and includes all known types of dinosaurs. It also shows the close relationship of birds (Aves) to dinosaurs.

SAUROPODOMORPHA

THEROPODA

SAURISCHIA

DINOSAURIA

ORNITHISCHIA

Dinosaur groups

All dinosaurs fall into one of two groups, or orders—Saurischia and Ornithischia. These in turn are subdivided into smaller groups right down to family level—a family is a group of dinosaur species with shared characteristics. Family names end in "idae." Where there is only one type, or genus, in a family the genus name is given instead of a family name and it is shown in *italics*. A broken line is shown for *Eoraptor*, which may be the earliest of all dinosaurs.

GENASAURIA

THYREOPHORA

CERAPODA

ORNITHOPODA

Nineteenth-century British paleontologist **Richard Owen** worked on a number of life-sized models of dinosaurs for an exhibition in London. In 1853, a special dinner held in his honor took place in the half-completed model of an *Iguanodon*.

A DINOSAUR FAMILY TREE

Eoraptor
Herrerasauridae
Ceratosauria
Abelisauridae
Podokesauridae
Megalosauridae
Compsognathus
Coelurus
Allosauridae
Spinosauridae
Dromaeosauridae
Other birds
Archaeopteryx
Oviraptoridae
Therizinosauridae
Tyrannosauridae
Troodontidae
Ornithomimidae
Thecodontosauridae
Plateosauridae
Melanorosauridae
Anchisauridae
Vulcanodontidae
Barapasaurus
Euhelopodidae
Cetiosauridae
Brachiosauridae
Camarasauridae
Titanosauridae
Nemegtosauridae
Diplodocidae
Pisanosaurus
Fabrosauridae
Scelidosauridae
Ankylosauridae
Nodosauridae
Stegosauria
Pachycephalosauridae
Homalocephalidae
Protoceratopsidae
Ceratopsidae
Psittacosauridae
Heterodontosauridae
Hypsilophodontidae
Iguanodontidae
Ouranosaurus
Hadrosauridae

AVES
MANIRAPTORA
TETANURAE
COELUROSAURIA
PACHYCEPHALOSAURIA
CERATOPSIA

57

Ceratosaurs

Ceratosaurs were meat-eating dinosaurs, ranging from tiny *Compsognathus* to large predators such as *Carnotaurus*. The group includes about 20 dinosaurs, the earliest known being *Coelophysis,* which dates from the Late Triassic. All walked upright on their back legs and had short arms. Several ceratosaurs had strangely shaped crests or horns on their heads. These were probably not used in battle, but in visual displays for attracting mates in the breeding season.

Herrerasaurus

(T) Late
Triassic

Size: 10 ft. (3 m) long
Order: Saurischia
Family: Herrerasauridae
Range: South America: Argentina
Pn: eh-ray-rah-SORE-us

Eoraptor

Ceratosaurus

With its powerful jaws armed with sharp, curved teeth, *Ceratosaurus* would have been a fierce hunter. On its short arms were hands with four strong clawed fingers and the long legs had three clawed toes on each foot. A row of bony plates ran down the center of the back and tail, and on its snout was a small horn. The horn seems to be too small to have been used for defense and may have been only for display.

(T) Late
Triassic

Size: 3¼ ft. (1 m) long
Order: Theropoda
Family: Eoraptoridae
Range: South America: Argentina
Pn: ee-oh-RAP-tor

Herrerasaurus

One of the earliest known dinosaurs, *Herrerasaurus* had a slender body and a long narrow head. It would have moved upright on its legs, which were more than twice the length of its arms. Its fingers were strong and had large curved claws for grasping prey. Sliding joints in the lower jaws allowed more flexibility when biting.

Eoraptor

Like *Herrerasaurus, Eoraptor* was one of the earliest known dinosaurs. It was also a carnivore but was smaller and more lightly built than its relative. Its teeth were sharp and slightly serrated for cutting through meat, but it did not have the flexible jaw joint of *Herrerasaurus.*

Ceratosaurus

(J) Late
Jurassic

Size: 20 ft. (6 m) long
Order: Saurischia
Family: Ceratosauridae
Range: North America: Colorado, Wyoming
Pn: SER-a-toe-SAW-rus

Compsognathus

One of the smallest of all dinosaurs, *Compsognathus* was probably not much bigger than a chicken. Its body was designed for speed, with lightweight bones, a long tail and long slender legs. Small reptiles were probably its main prey—the remains of a lizard were found in one fossilized skeleton of *Compsognathus*.

Compsognathus

J Late Jurassic

Size: 24 in. (60 cm) long
Order: Saurischia
Family: Compsognathidae
Range: Europe: Germany, France
Pn: komp-soh-NAY-thus

Dilophosaurus

J Early Jurassic

Size: 20 ft. (6 m) long
Order: Saurischia
Family: Ceratosauridae
Range: North America: Arizona
Pn: die-LOAF-oh-SAW-rus

Dilophosaurus

This dinosaur had a pair of semicircular bony crests, one on each side of its skull. Some experts believe that only the males had these crests and that they were used in displays to attract females. Its teeth were sharp but slender, suggesting that this dinosaur may have killed its prey with its clawed feet and hands rather than with its jaws.

Coelophysis

T Late Triassic

Size: up to 10 ft. (3 m) long
Order: Saurischia
Family: Podokesauridae
Range: North America: Connecticut, New Mexico
Pn: seel-oh-FY-sis

Coelophysis

Built for speed, *Coelophysis* had a light slender body and long slim legs and tail. The narrow jaws were lined with sharp serrated teeth for attacking prey. Remains of more than 1,000 skeletons were found in New Mexico, suggesting that this dinosaur lived in herds.

Carnotaurus

Cr Mid to Late Cretaceous

Size: 24½ ft. (7.5 m) long
Order: Saurischia
Family: Abelisauridae
Range: South America: Argentina
Pn: kar-noh-TORE-us

Carnotaurus

Discovered in 1985, this dinosaur had a deep, bull-like head with big horns above the eyes—its name means "meat-eating bull." Its arms were extremely small and probably almost useless. Well-preserved skin impressions found near the bones show that small cone-shaped spines covered the sides of its body.

Attacking Dinosaurs

Just like animals today, predatory dinosaurs engaged in life and death struggles with their prey. Special weapons, such as powerful claws, sharp teeth, and strong jaws, helped them win their battles. Speed was also important to an attacking dinosaur. Smaller hunters, in particular, relied on being able to get close to their victims in high-speed chases before making the final pounce. Larger predators, such as tyrannosaurs, relied on their size and strength to overcome their prey.

Hunting in packs

Smaller hunting dinosaurs such as *Deinonychus* and *Dromaeosaurus* may have hunted in packs to bring down huge plant eaters much larger than themselves. Like hunting dogs today, a group of predators could have surrounded a large dinosaur, some leaping on its back while others slashed at its skin with their sharp claws.

Speedy hunter

Dromaeosaurus lived in North America during the late Cretaceous period. A slender-bodied dinosaur, it ran fast on two legs and may have reached speeds of 37 mph (60 km/h) or more. When it caught up with its prey, it leaped off the ground to tear at the victim's flesh using the powerful claws on its back feet. The long tail helped *Dromaeosaurus* balance as it ran and pounce on its prey.

Dromaeosaurus

Each hand had three sharp-clawed fingers which *Dromaeosaurus* used to seize hold of its prey.

Springs toward its victim

Dromaeosaurus chases prey

Leaps off ground to tear at prey's flesh

Special weapons

Dromaeosaurus had a lethal weapon—an extra-large claw on the second toe of each foot. This sharp, curving claw measured up to 5 in. (13 cm) long. When running, *Dromaeosaurus* held these special weapons off the ground so they did not become damaged or blunt. But when the dinosaur attacked, it used its powerful claws to slash and hack at its victim.

Dromaeosaurus

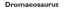

Dinosaur diets

In the time of the dinosaurs, just like today, there were far more plant-eating animals than meat eaters. Only the largest hunters, such as tyrannosaurs, would have dared tackle the biggest plant eaters, and even then they would probably have chosen a young or injured animal to attack. The smallest meat eaters probably relied on catching lizards and insects for the bulk of their food, while Dromaeosaurs and their relatives may have hunted in packs to bring down creatures much larger than themselves. At least one dinosaur, the long-jawed *Baryonyx*, may have preyed mainly on fish.

Powerful jaws

A fierce hunter, *Deinonychus* had a large head and extremely powerful jaws. The jaws were lined with backward-curving teeth which had jagged edges like a bread knife for slicing into the flesh of its prey. At 10–13 ft. (3–4 m) long, *Deinonychus* was twice as big as its relative *Dromaeosaurus*. It, too, had a lethal claw on the second toe of each foot.

Ornitholestes

Deinonychus

A fast-moving hunter, *Ornitholestes* (left) lived in North America during the late Jurassic. It probably preyed on lizards and frogs as well as insects and the earliest birds.

Tetanurans

Allosaurus

The tetanurans were a group of large predatory dinosaurs that lived in the Jurassic and Cretaceous periods. Despite their appearance, these dinosaurs were closely related to birds. They included groups such as the allosaurs and megalosaurs as well as a number of more recently discovered dinosaurs such as *Giganotosaurus*. All the tetanurans had a large opening in each upper jaw bone that made the skull much lighter than it looks. The rear part of the tail was stiffened by special interlocking bony structures on the vertebrae— the name tetanuran means "stiff tail."

Allosaurus

Mighty *Allosaurus* probably weighed between 1 and 2 tons and stood about 15 ft. (4.5 m) tall. Packs of these fierce dinosaurs may have hunted together so they could bring down even larger creatures, such as sauropods and stegosaurs.

J Late Jurassic

Size: up to 33 ft. (10 m) long
Order: Saurischia
Family: Allosauridae
Range: Asia: China
Pn: yang-choo-AN-oh-SAW-rus

Yangchuanosaurus

Yangchuanosaurus

This dinosaur was first discovered in China in 1978. A typical allosaur, it had a huge head, powerful jaws and jagged-edged teeth. Its long tail made up about half of its body length and helped to balance the heavy body as the dinosaur strode along on its sturdy legs.

Giganotosaurus

Cr Late Cretaceous

Size: 43 ft. (13 m) long
Order: Saurischia
Family: Abelisauridae
Range: South America: Patagonia
Pn: jig-a-NOT-o-SAW-rus

Giganotosaurus

First discovered in South America in 1993, *Giganotosaurus* was one of the largest of all meat-eating dinosaurs. It may have weighed as much as 8 tons. As well as hunting its own prey, it may have scared other predators away and stolen their catches.

Size: up to 39 ft. (12 m) long

Order: Saurischia

Family: Allosauridae

Range: North America: Colorado, Utah, Wyoming; Africa: Tanzania; Australia

Pn: AL-oh-SAW-rus

J Jurassic

Size: 30 ft. (9 m) long

Order: Saurischia

Family: Megalosauridae

Range: Europe: England, France; Africa: Morocco

Pn: MEG-ah-loh-SAW-rus

Cr Early Cretaceous

Size: 26 ft. (8 m) long

Order: Saurischia

Family: uncertain

Range: Africa: Egypt, Morocco, Tunisia

Pn: kar-kar-o-DON-toh-SAW-rus

Carcharodontosaurus

In 1996, scientists discovered fossils of a giant meat-eating dinosaur in the Moroccan desert. Its skull alone measured more than 5 ft. (1.5 m) and was longer than that of *Tyrannosaurus*. Its teeth were 5 in. (12 cm) long, giving this dinosaur its name, which means "shark-toothed reptile."

Cryolophosaurus

This large meat eater was discovered in Antarctica in 1994. It had a unique crest which ran across its skull, with two small horns on each side. The crest was too thin to have been a weapon so experts think that it was probably used for display during the mating season.

Cryolophosaurus

Megalosaurus

This was the first dinosaur to be scientifically named in England, in 1824. A typical meat eater, it had a large head, powerful jaws and curved, saw-edged teeth. With its strong, clawed fingers and toes, it was well equipped to attack large plant-eating dinosaurs.

Megalosaurus

Suchomimus

Fossils of this dinosaur were discovered in 1998 in the Sahara Desert. A member of a group of fish-eating dinosaurs called spinosaurs, it had a long narrow snout like a crocodile and thumb claws measuring 12 in. (30 cm).

Cr Early Cretaceous

Size: 33 ft. (10 m) long

Order: Saurischia

Family: Spinosauridae

Range: Africa: Niger

Pn: SOOK-o-MEEM-us

J Early Jurassic

Size: 23–26 ft. (7–8 m) long

Order: Saurischia

Family: uncertain

Range: Antarctica

Pn: cry-oh-LOAF-oh-SAW-rus

Suchomimus

63

Finding a Mate

No one can ever know exactly how dinosaurs went about finding their partners, but experts can make some good guesses based on fossil evidence and on the behavior of similar animals today. Some male dinosaurs may have had brightly colored skin that helped them to attract females, just as many birds today attract mates by showing off their colorful feathers. The strangely shaped horns and crests of other dinosaurs may also have been used in courtship displays. Dinosaurs such as *Triceratops* may have locked horns in battles over mates just like deer do today. The large bony neck frills of many horned dinosaurs made them look bigger than they were and may have helped males to impress females.

Mating calls

Parasaurolophus, like many duckbilled dinosaurs, had a tall crest on the top of its head. The crest was hollow inside and may have acted like an echo chamber to make the dinosaur's booming call louder. This call may have been used to keep in touch with other members of the herd or to attract females. The dinosaur could also have shown off its splendid crest in a visual display to females. Experts do not know whether female duckbills had smaller crests or any crests at all.

Parasaurolophus

The hornlike crest on the head of the duckbilled dinosaur *Parasaurolophus* was nearly 6½ ft. (2 m) long.

Colorful markings

In the early days of dinosaur study, dinosaurs were thought to be drab brown and gray. Now more people believe that they may have been brightly colored—just like some reptiles today. And perhaps these colorful markings, such as those of *Yangchuanosaurus*, could have been displayed to attract mates in the breeding season.

Yangchuanosaurus

Dilophosaurus

Crest display

A fast-moving, meat-eating dinosaur, *Dilophosaurus* had two bony, semicircular crests on the top of its head. They were too thin to have been used for attack or defense, so experts believe the crests may have been shown off in courtship displays to help *Dilophosaurus* to attract mates.

Battles

On the head of bonehead dinosaurs such as *Stegoceras* was a high dome of thickened bone. Some dinosaur experts think rival males took part in head-butting battles to win females. The dinosaurs may have charged toward one another with their heads lowered and tails held out. The domed area of the skull would have taken most of the impact as the animals crashed into each other.

Stegoceras

Male *Stegoceras* dinosaurs probably had bigger domes than females, and experts think that the domes grew bigger with age.

Early Jurassic Seas

In the Jurassic period, which began about 208 million years ago, the oceans of the world were filled with a wide range of creatures. The feathery crinoids that sprouted from the sea floor were not plants, but animals that lived attached to the seabed. Ammonites and belemnites—relatives of today's octopus and squid—as well as many kinds of fish, were preyed on by huge marine reptiles such as icthyosaurs.

Ichthyosaurus

Eurhinosaurus

Ammonite

Temnodontosaurus

Pholidophorus

Dapedium

Belemnite

Crinoid

67

Jurassic Times

During the Jurassic period, the climate became wetter and thick plants, such as ferns, conifers, and ginkgos, covered much of the land. New kinds of dinosaurs developed, feeding on the lush plant life. These included sauropods, which were the biggest creatures ever to live on land; they ate more than 1 ton of plant food a day. Plentiful prey also allowed more types of meat-eating dinosaur to thrive. In the air were flying insects and pterosaurs, as well as the first species of birds.

Shunosaurus, a sauropod

Ginkgo

Tree fern

Frog

The Jurassic world

During the Jurassic period the supercontinent of Pangaea split into two, creating the land areas of Laurasia in the north and Gondwana in the south. The climate was still warm all over the world but rainfall increased.

Siberia
LAURASIA
China
Europe
NORTH AMERICA
Turkey
Iran
Tibet
Spain
PACIFIC OCEAN
TETHYS OCEAN
EQUATOR
South America
Africa
southwest China
GONDWANA
India
Australia
Antarctica

Key to map

- Ocean
- Landmass
- Sea-covered continent

Mid Jurassic China

In this mid-Jurassic scene in what is now southwest China, a stegosaur, *Huayangosaurus*, rears back in fear as fast-moving meat eaters, *Gasosaurus*, approach. Sauropods, *Shunosaurus*, look up from feeding on tree ferns—despite their great bulk even they could fall prey to a group of these sharp-toothed predators.

Angustinaripterus, a flying reptile (pterosaur)

Ginkgo

Conifer

Gasosaurus, a tetanuran

Cycad

Huayangosaurus, a stegosaur

Fern

Salamander

Horsetails

69

Late Jurassic

In the warm wet climate of the late Jurassic, plants thrived. In this European forest are huge redwood trees as well as cycads, horsetails, and ferns. The plants provided food for dinosaurs such as *Cetiosaurus* and *Camptosaurus*, while flying reptiles such as *Scaphognathus* and the earliest known bird, *Archaeopteryx*, may have fed on insects. However, powerful killers, such as *Megalosaurus*, preyed on plant-eating dinosaurs.

Cetiosaurus

Archaeopteryx

Camptosaurus

Fern

Cycad

Megalosaurus

Archaeopteryx

Bird Relatives

This group, known as the Maniraptora, includes several types of birdlike dinosaur, such as dromaeosaurs and troodontids, as well as birds themselves. A feature shared by all of these creatures was a special flexible wrist joint that allowed the front limb to be folded against the body. The dinosaurs in this group were probably all fast-moving hunters that ran on two legs. *Archaeopteryx*, the earliest known bird, lived about 150 million years ago and had features of both birds and reptiles. Like birds today, it had wings and a covering of feathers. But like reptiles, it had toothed jaws and a long bony tail.

Stenonychosaurus

Compared to its body size, *Stenonychosaurus* had the biggest brain of any dinosaur. It also had large eyes, measuring about 2 in. (5 cm) across. A slender creature, built for fast running, it probably hunted at night.

Cr Late Cretaceous

Size: 6½ ft. (2 m) long
Order: Saurischia
Family: Troodontidae
Range: North America: Alberta
Pn: STEN-oh-nike-o-SAW-rus

Velociraptor

Stenonychosaurus

Cr Late Cretaceous

Size: 6 ft. (1.8 m) long
Order: Saurischia
Family: Dromaeosauridae
Range: Asia: Mongolia, China
Pn: vel-O-si-RAP-tor

Velociraptor

A fast-moving hunter, *Velociraptor* had a long, flat-snouted head. Two fossilized skeletons found in Mongolia revealed *Velociraptor* locked in battle with a horned dinosaur, *Protoceratops* (see page 129). Scientists think that the two may have died in a sandstorm that developed during the attack.

Archaeopteryx

Archaeopteryx

Unlike birds today, *Archaeopteryx* did not have a large breastbone to support powerful flying muscles. It probably could not fly far and may have had to climb up trees in order to launch itself into the air and then flap and glide short distances in search of insect prey.

J Late Jurassic

Size: 14 in. (35 cm) long
Order: Saurischia: Aves
Family: Archaeopterygidae
Range: Europe: Germany
Pn: ark-ee-OP-ter-iks

72

Deinonychus

A fast, agile predator, *Deinonychus* had a special weapon. The second toe on each foot bore a large curved claw, 5 in. (12 cm) long. The dinosaur could have stood on one leg and used the claw of the other foot to slash into its victim's flesh.

Cr Early Cretaceous

Size: 10–13 ft. (3–4 m) long
Order: Saurischia
Family: Dromaeosauridae
Range: North America: Montana
Pn: die-NON-i-kus

Deinonychus

Dromaeosaurus

Like *Deinonychus*, this dinosaur had large, curved claws on its feet that it used as weapons to kill prey. This fierce, fast-moving creature probably hunted in packs that could have brought down animals much larger than themselves.

Saurornithoides

Like *Stenonychosaurus*, this dinosaur had a big brain and probably had well-developed senses. Its eyes were large, suggesting that it may have been active at night, coming out to hunt small reptiles and other creatures.

Cr Late Cretaceous

Size: 6½ ft. (2 m) long
Order: Saurischia
Family: Troodontidae
Range: Asia: Mongolia
Pn: sore-OR-nith-oid-eez

Saurornithoides

Scipionyx

This creature was only named as a dinosaur in 1998, although the fossil was discovered 10 years earlier. The fossil is unique in that it contains parts of the gut—the first ever evidence of the internal organs of a dinosaur. *Scipionyx* was probably a meat eater and ran upright on two legs.

Cr Late Cretaceous

Size: 6 ft. (1.8 m) long
Order: Saurischia
Family: Dromaeosauridae
Range: North America: Alberta
Pn: DROH-may-oh-SORE-us

Cr Early Cretaceous

Size: 20–39 in. (50 cm–1 m) long
Order: Saurischia
Family: uncertain
Range: Europe: Italy
Pn: skip-ee-OH-nix

Dromaeosaurus

Scipionyx

Ostrich Dinosaurs

With their slender legs, long necks, and small heads, the ostrich dinosaurs looked similar to the ostriches of today. Like ostriches, the ostrich dinosaurs were fast runners and may have been able to sprint along at up to 40 mph (65 km/h) as they searched for food such as lizards and frogs. They may also have eaten leaves and fruit, which they could have pulled from the trees with the slender clawed fingers on their hands. Possible relatives of the ornithomimids are the therizinosaurids (also known as segnosaurids). Complete skeletons of these creatures have only recently been discovered. Unlike other theropods, they probably fed on plants.

Ornithomimus

A typical ostrich dinosaur, *Ornithomimus* had a lightly built body and slender back legs. As it ran, the dinosaur would have held its long tail straight out behind to help balance the weight of its body. It had no teeth but it used its hard beak to chop its food into pieces that it could swallow.

Ornithomimus

(Cr) Late Cretaceous

Size: 11½ ft. (3.5 m) long
Order: Saurischia
Family: Ornithomimidae
Range: North America: Colorado, Montana; Asia: Tibet
Pn: or-NITH-oh-MEEM-us

Dromiceiomimus

Oviraptor

The name of this dinosaur means "egg thief" because the first fossil was found with a clutch of eggs. It was thought that these belonged to another dinosaur and that *Oviraptor* was raiding the nest. Now scientists have discovered that the eggs belonged to *Oviraptor* and it probably died defending its eggs.

(Cr) Late Cretaceous

Size: 6 ft. (1.8 m) long
Order: Saurischia
Family: Oviraptoridae
Range: Asia: Mongolia
Pn: OHV-ih-RAP-tor

Dromiceiomimus

Skulls of this ostrich dinosaur show that it had a huge brain and large eyes—larger than those of any modern land animal. It probably hunted at night, catching small mammals and lizards in its toothless beak. Its legs were particularly long so it was probably a very fast runner.

(Cr) Late Cretaceous

Size: 11½ ft. (3.5 m) long
Order: Saurischia
Family: Ornithomimidae
Range: North America: Alberta
Pn: droh-MEE-see-oh-MEEM-us

Oviraptor

Pelecanimimus

This was the first ostrich dinosaur to be discovered in Europe. It had a long narrow skull and fossil impressions reveal that it may have had a throat pouch like a pelican. Unlike other ostrich dinosaurs, *Pelecanimimus* had a large number of teeth in its long jaws—as many as 220.

Pelecanimimus

Cr Early Cretaceous

Size: up to 6½ ft. (2 m) long
Order: Saurischia
Family: Ornithomimidae
Range: Europe: Spain
Pn: pel-e-KAN-i-MEEM-us

Therizinosaurus

The few fossils that have been found so far of *Therizinosaurus* show a creature with arms bearing huge sickle-shaped claws more than 27 in. (70 cm) long. The dinosaur may have used these claws to gather leaves and pass them to its toothless beak.

Therizinosaurus

Cr Late Cretaceous

Size: 13–16 ft. (4–5 m) long
Order: Saurischia
Family: Therizinosauridae
Range: Asia: Mongolia, China
Pn: thair-uh-ZEEN-uh-SAW-rus

Alxasaurus

Cr Early Cretaceous

Size: up to 13 ft. (4 m) long
Order: Saurischia
Family: Therizinosauridae
Range: Asia: Mongolia, China
Pn: AHL-shah-SAW-rus

Alxasaurus

A relative of *Therizinosaurus*, *Alxasaurus* also had long slender arms and hands with huge claws. Its body was bulky with large hips and a short tail, which it may have used to help prop itself up as it fed. The small head ended in a toothless beak, but there were some small teeth farther back in the jaws.

Gallimimus

Gallimimus

One of the largest of the ostrich dinosaurs, *Gallimimus* was twice the size of a modern ostrich. Like the rest of its group, it did not have strong teeth or sharp claws to defend itself from attackers. Instead it relied on speed—few other dinosaurs could catch it when it ran.

Cr Late Cretaceous

Size: 13 ft. (4 m) long
Order: Saurischia
Family: Ornithomimidae
Range: Asia: Mongolia
Pn: gal-lee-MEEM-us

Tyrannosaurs

Huge, flesh-eating dinosaurs, tyrannosaurs lived in Asia and North America during the Late Cretaceous. They were among the largest land carnivores that have ever lived. All tyrannosaurs had massive heads and strong jaws lined with sharp teeth, some of which were up to 6 in. (15 cm) long. They walked upright on their two back legs and could probably move at 20 mph (30 km/h) or more. Their front limbs were so small they did not even reach the mouth. Some experts think that a tyrannosaur may have used its tiny arms to lift itself off the ground after sleeping or feeding.

Siamotyrannus

First discovered in Thailand in 1996, this creature may be the oldest known tyrannosaur. It lived some 50 million years before *Tyrannosaurus*. Like its relative, *Siamotyrannus* had jagged, curved teeth and probably fed on plant-eating dinosaurs much larger than itself.

Siamotyrannus

Daspletosaurus

Cr Early Cretaceous

Size: 16–23 ft. (5–7 m) long
Order: Saurischia
Family: Tyrannosauridae
Range: Asia: Thailand
Pn: sigh-AM-oh-TIE-ran-us

Cr Late Cretaceous

Size: 28 ft. (8.5 m) long
Order: Saurischia
Family: Tyrannosauridae
Range: North America: Alberta
Pn: das-PLEE-toh-SAW-rus

Alioramus

While most tyrannosaurs had deep skulls and short snouts, *Alioramus* had a long narrow skull. There were also a number of bony knobs on the snout and near the eyes. Like other tyrannosaurs, it may have lain in wait for prey, ready to pounce when the victim came near.

Alioramus

Cr Late Cretaceous

Size: 20 ft. (6 m) long
Order: Saurischia
Family: Tyrannosauridae
Range: Asia: Mongolia
Pn: ay-lee-oh-RAY-mus

Daspletosaurus

Although this dinosaur was smaller than *Tyrannosaurus*, it was still a fierce hunter. Equipped with large, saw-edged teeth, clawed feet and a powerful body, *Daspletosaurus* could have hunted the large horned dinosaurs that lived in the North American forests at the time.

Tarbosaurus

Cr Late
Cretaceous

Size: 46 ft. (14 m) long
Order: Saurischia
Family: Tyrannosauridae
Range: Asia: Mongolia
Pn: TAR-boh-SAW-rus

Albertosaurus

Like all tyrannosaurs, *Albertosaurus* had a second set of ribs lining its belly. These extra ribs may have helped to support its insides so that they were not crushed by the animal's huge weight when it lay down. A fierce hunter, *Albertosaurus* could have killed its prey with a bite to the neck.

Albertosaurus

Tarbosaurus

Like all tyrannosaurs, *Tarbosaurus* had small, weak front limbs. There were two fingers on each hand, each bearing a claw. The legs and feet were large and bulky, with four toes on each foot. Three of these pointed forward and the fourth, much smaller, toe was directed backward. This fearsome creature could have driven other hunters away from their kills as well as hunting its own prey.

Cr Late
Cretaceous

Size: 26 ft. (8 m) long
Order: Saurischia
Family: Tyrannosauridae
Range: North America: Alberta
Pn: al-BERT-oh-SAW-rus

Tyrannosaurus

Up to 20 ft. (6 m) tall and weighing more than an African elephant, *Tyrannosaurus* was one of the most fearsome creatures of the Cretaceous. Some scientists think that its bulk may have made it hard to chase prey, and that it scavenged for food, eating animals that were already dead. In fact, like lions today, *Tyrannosaurus* probably hunted and scavenged.

Cr Late
Cretaceous

Size: up to 49 ft. (15 m) long
Order: Saurischia
Family: Tyrannosauridae
Range: North America: Alberta,
Montana, Saskatchewan, Texas,
Wyoming; Asia: Mongolia
Pn: tie-RAN-oh-SAW-rus

Tyrannosaurus

Tyrannosaurus

As one of the biggest hunters that has ever lived on land, *Tyrannosaurus* was the king of the Cretaceous. Scientists have discovered more than 20 skeletons of this huge killer, and it is one of the best known of all dinosaurs. *Tyrannosaurus* ran upright on its two back legs, but with its huge bulk it could not have moved fast for long. Instead it probably relied on staying hidden until it was close enough to its prey to make a sudden surprise pounce. *Tyrannosaurus* killed its victims with vicious bites to the neck with its long, bladelike teeth.

Lethal weapons

The mighty skull of *Tyrannosaurus* was more than a 3 ft (1 m) long. Lining its jaws were more than 60 razor-sharp teeth, some of which were as much as 6 in. (15 cm) long. With these lethal weapons, *Tyrannosaurus* could kill and rip apart a large plant eater in seconds. Its bite was probably more powerful than that of any other dinosaur, capable of crushing even the bones of its prey.

Scavenging for food

Like many large carnivores today, *Tyrannosaurus* may have eaten carrion—animals that were already dead—as well as killing its own prey. It may also have driven smaller meat-eating dinosaurs from their kills and feasted on the remains.

Tyrannosaurus discoveries

Most *Tyrannosaurus* fossils have been found in the western part of North America. The first was discovered by American fossil hunter Barnum Brown in 1902. The dinosaur was then named in 1905 by an American palaeontologist, Henry Fairfield Osborn—the name *Tyrannosaurus* means "tyrant lizard." One of the biggest *Tyrannosaurus* fossil discoveries was an almost complete skeleton found in South Dakota, in 1990. Nicknamed Sue after its discoverer, the fossilized bones were sold in 1997 to a Chicago museum for $7.6 million dollars.

Meat Eaters

Tracking down and killing prey takes more effort than feeding on plants, but one good meal would have satisfied a meat-eating dinosaur for several days. Meat eaters were usually fast runners so they could chase their prey. They also had special weapons such as sharp teeth and long claws for killing and tearing apart their victims. Just like hunting animals today, most meat-eating dinosaurs would have had good eyesight and a keen sense of smell to help them find their prey.

Dinosaur diets

Meat-eating dinosaurs hunted the plant eaters that lived around them—just like lions and other carnivores today. But there is little real evidence of what dinosaurs ate. Some fossilized dung—called coprolites—has been found, and specimens almost certainly from a *Tyrannosaurus* show the crushed bones of its prey. Fossilized stomach contents have occasionally been discovered. *Baryonyx* fossils, for example, contained fish scales, and a *Sinosauropteryx* fossil revealed the remains of a small mammal.

Hunting prey

In this Late Cretaceous scene in what is now known as Mongolia, a large tyrannosaur (*Tarbosaurus*) is chasing an ostrich dinosaur (*Gallimimus*). Thanks to its speed, *Gallimimus* may be able to escape the tyrannosaur's jaws. Another small dinosaur, the one-fingered *Mononykus*, runs from the predator. Nearby a much smaller meat eater, *Velociraptor*, attacks *Oviraptor*. Both are about the same size, but *Velociraptor* has sharp curving toe claws for use as weapons.

Tarbosaurus

Gallimimus

Mononykus

Designed for killing

The largest hunters, such as tyrannosaurs, were the top
predators of their time. They were built for power and
strength, able to run fast for a short time, seize prey in
their powerful jaws, and kill it with vicious bites
from their long serrated teeth.

Meat eater's skull

Tyrannosaurus

The jaws of a meat eater were lined with sharp teeth,
which curved backward and had serrated edges for
slicing into the flesh of prey.

Protoceratops

Velociraptor

Oviraptor

Velociraptor bites into the neck of
Oviraptor while tearing at its victim's
flesh with its sharp toe claws.

Oviraptor

81

Plant Eaters

What did dinosaurs eat? Like large animals today, some dinosaurs were plant eaters, while others would have hunted and killed other creatures. There would have been many more plant-eating dinosaurs than flesh eaters, but they may have avoided competing with one another by feeding at different levels. Small dinosaurs, such as *Protoceratops*, would have grazed at ground level. Larger horned dinosaurs could have fed on low bushes. Duckbilled dinosaurs could have reared up on their hind legs while feeding to reach leaves higher in the trees. Biggest of all the plant eaters were the mighty sauropods. They could stretch up to eat the fresh growth at the very tops of trees where no other creatures could reach.

Triceratops

Protoceratops

Sharing resources

Here a group of plant-eating dinosaurs, ranging from a small horned dinosaur to a giant sauropod, feed together, each at its own level. The largest dinosaurs would have had to eat huge quantities of plants every day to get enough nourishment. A sauropod might have eaten as much as 1 ton of leaves a day.

The fossilized droppings of dinosaurs are known as coprolites and provide valuable clues about what dinosaurs ate. Coprolites that have been studied show the remains of plant material such as conifer stems and cycad leaves. But although experts can tell what a dropping contains, it is hard to know which species of dinosaur it came from.

Alamosaurus

Coprolites

Camarasaurus

Edmontosaurus

Edmontosaurus

Sauropod teeth

The various plant eaters had different types of teeth to deal with the food they ate. Sauropods such as *Camarasaurus* (above) had peglike teeth for stripping leaves and shoots from trees.

Toothless beaks

Duckbilled dinosaurs and horned dinosaurs both had a toothless beak at the front of the jaws for chopping off mouthfuls of tough ferns and other plants. The food was then ground down with broad, flat teeth farther back in the jaws.

Triceratops

83

Prosauropods

This group of long-necked dinosaurs first appeared in the Late Triassic. There were two main groups—the plateosaurids, which had large, heavy bodies, and the anchisaurids, which were smaller and more lightly built. Like the later sauropods, prosauropods are thought to have been plant eaters. Although these dinosaurs have some similarities to sauropods, they are not an early form of sauropod as their name suggests. They are probably a side branch of the group and they had died out by the end of the Early Jurassic.

Plateosaurus

Anchisaurus

A small, lightly built prosauropod, *Anchisaurus* had a small head, long neck and slender body. Its arms were shorter than its legs and it probably moved on two legs as well as four. On its thumb was a large claw, which the dinosaur may have used for uprooting plants or for defending itself.

J Early Jurassic

Size: 7 ft. (2.1 m) long
Order: Saurischia
Family: Anchisauridae
Range: North America: Connecticut; southern Africa
Pn: AN-ki-SAW-rus

Anchisaurus

T Late Triassic   **J** Early Jurassic

Size: 33 ft. (10 m) long
Order: Saurischia
Family: Melanorosauridae
Range: South America: Argentina
Pn: ree-O-ha-SAW-rus

Riojasaurus

Riojasaurus

A large, bulky dinosaur, *Riojasaurus* was too heavy to rear up on to two legs. It would have had to walk on all fours in order to support its body weight. It is named after La Rioja Province in Argentina, where its fossils were found.

Plateosaurus

Many well-preserved skeletons of *Plateosaurus* have been discovered, making this the best known of the prosauropods. The tail made up about half the length of this large animal. It had a strong head and many small leaf-shaped teeth for feeding on plants. It would have moved on all fours for much of the time, but could have reared up on two legs to browse on the leaves of tall trees.

T Late Triassic

Size: up to 23 ft. (7 m) long
Order: Saurischia
Family: Plateosauridae
Range: Europe: England, France, Germany, Switzerland
Pn: PLAT-ee-oh-SAW-rus

Lufengosaurus

J Early Jurassic

Size: 16–23 ft. (5–7 m) long
Order: Saurischia
Family: Plateosauridae
Range: Asia: China
Pn: loo-FUNG-oh-SAW-rus

Lufengosaurus

Some 30 skeletons of this prosauropod have been discovered to date and *Lufengosaurus* was the first complete dinosaur to be mounted and displayed in China. It also appeared on the first ever dinosaur postage stamp, issued in China in 1958. A large, heavily built animal, *Lufengosaurus* had large hands, broad feet, and widely spaced teeth.

T Late Triassic

Size: 13 ft. (4 m) long
Order: Saurischia
Family: Plateosauridae
Range: North America: Arizona; Africa: South Africa, Zimbabwe
Pn: MASS-oh-SPOND-ih-lus

Massospondylus

Massospondylus

Massospondylus had a small head on a very long, flexible neck. Its large, five-fingered hands could have been used for collecting food or for walking when on all fours. Stones have been found with some skeletons—the dinosaur probably swallowed these to help it grind down tough plants in the stomach.

T Late Triassic **J** Early Jurassic

Size: 10 ft. (3 m) long
Order: Saurischia
Family: Plateosauridae
Range: South America: Argentina
Pn: moo-SAW-rus

Mussaurus

In 1979, a group of tiny *Mussaurus* hatchlings were found in a nest in Argentina. Two small eggs lay nearby, each measuring only 1 in. (2.5 cm) long. Other skeletons found were about 12 in. (30 cm) long and probably belonged to young animals.

Mussaurus

Thecodontosaurus

Like *Anchisaurus*, this dinosaur was lightly built, but it had a shorter neck and more teeth than its relative. It was first named in 1842 after its fossilized bones were found in southwest England.

T Late Triassic **J** Early Jurassic

Size: 7 ft. (2.1m) long
Order: Saurischia
Family: Anchisauridae
Range: Europe: England; southern Africa
Pn: THEEK-oh-don-toe-SAW-rus

Thecodontosaurus

Sauropods

These long-necked, plant-eating dinosaurs were the largest land animals ever known. The smallest were at least 33 ft. (10 m) long and the largest may have measured as much as 125 ft. (38 m). All were similar in appearance, with a small head on a long neck, a deep body, thick pillarlike legs, and a long tapering tail. They walked on all fours and were probably slow moving. There were several different families of sauropods.

Brachiosaurs were some of the biggest and heaviest, while diplodocids, such as *Seismosaurus*, were even longer, but had lighter bones.

Cr Late Cretaceous

Size: 39 ft. (12 m) long
Order: Saurischia
Family: Titanosauridae
Range: South America: Argentina
Pn: SALT-a-SAW-rus

Saltasaurus

Saltasaurus

Titanosaurs such as *Saltasaurus* first appeared in the Late Jurassic and survived until the end of the Cretaceous period. *Saltasaurus* was one of the smaller species. Set into its skin were a large number of small bony plates, some bearing spikes, which would have helped defend this plant eater against its flesh-eating enemies.

J Late Jurassic

Size: 49 ft. (15 m) long
Order: Saurischia
Family: Camarasauridae
Range: Asia: China
Pn: yoo-HEL-oh-pus

Euhelopus

Euhelopus

Euhelopus was a close relative of *Camarasaurus*, although it lived on the other side of the world. Its body shape was very similar, but its neck was much longer and contained as many as 17 to 19 vertebrae. (*Camarasaurus* had only 12 vertebrae.) Its teeth were large and spoon shaped, suitable for eating tough plants such as ferns and horsetails.

Alamosaurus

Alamosaurus was one of the last titanosaurs and lived right at the end of the Late Cretaceous. Like others in its family, it had a broad snout with slender teeth that could have been used to strip leaves from branches. It is named after the Alamo, the famous fortress that the Texans held against a Mexican siege in 1836. The first specimens were found in Ojo Alamo, in New Mexico.

Cr Late Cretaceous

Size: 69 ft. (21 m) long
Order: Saurischia
Family: Titanosauridae
Range: North America: Montana, New Mexico, Texas, Utah
Pn: AL-am-oh-SAW-rus

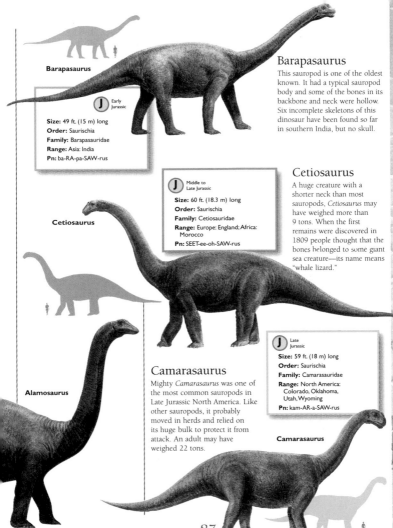

Barapasaurus

J Early Jurassic

Size: 49 ft. (15 m) long
Order: Saurischia
Family: Barapasauridae
Range: Asia: India
Pn: ba-RA-pa-SAW-rus

Barapasaurus

This sauropod is one of the oldest known. It had a typical sauropod body and some of the bones in its backbone and neck were hollow. Six incomplete skeletons of this dinosaur have been found so far in southern India, but no skull.

Cetiosaurus

J Middle to Late Jurassic

Size: 60 ft. (18.3 m) long
Order: Saurischia
Family: Cetiosauridae
Range: Europe: England; Africa: Morocco
Pn: SEET-ee-oh-SAW-rus

Cetiosaurus

A huge creature with a shorter neck than most sauropods, *Cetiosaurus* may have weighed more than 9 tons. When the first remains were discovered in 1809 people thought that the bones belonged to some giant sea creature—its name means "whale lizard."

Alamosaurus

J Late Jurassic

Size: 59 ft. (18 m) long
Order: Saurischia
Family: Camarasauridae
Range: North America: Colorado, Oklahoma, Utah, Wyoming
Pn: kam-AR-a-SAW-rus

Camarasaurus

Mighty *Camarasaurus* was one of the most common sauropods in Late Jurassic North America. Like other sauropods, it probably moved in herds and relied on its huge bulk to protect it from attack. An adult may have weighed 22 tons.

Camarasaurus

Diplodocus

Diplodocus

This huge animal's neck was 24 ft. (7.3 m) long but, at only 24 in. (60 cm), its head was not much bigger than a horse's. Despite its size, *Diplodocus* weighed only 11 tons, much less than *Brachiosaurus*. This was because its vertebrae were partly hollow. Its tail was made up of at least 70 bones and was probably held off the ground as it walked.

J Late Jurassic

Size: 85 ft. (26 m) long
Order: Saurischia
Family: Diplodocidae
Range: North America: Colorado, Montana, Utah, Wyoming
Pn: dip-LOD-oh-kus

Brachiosaurus

Brachiosaurus

This giant may have weighed 88 tons, more than 12 African elephants. Like a giraffe, it had a very long neck and front legs that were longer than its back legs so that the body sloped down from the shoulders. It probably fed like a giraffe, too, reaching up to eat leaves on the highest trees.

J Late Jurassic

Size: 75 ft. (23 m) long
Order: Saurischia
Family: Brachiosauridae
Range: North America: Colorado; Africa: Tanzania, Algeria
Pn: BRACK-ee-oh-SAW-rus

J Late Jurassic

Size: 72 ft. (22 m) long
Order: Saurischia
Family: Diplodocidae
Range: Asia: Mongolia
Pn: ma-MENCH-ih-SAW-rus

Mamenchisaurus

J Late Jurassic

Size: 125 ft. (38 m) long
Order: Saurischia
Family: Diplodocidae
Range: North America: New Mexico
Pn: SIZE-moh-SAW-rus

Dicraeosaurus

Dicraeosaurus

Dicraeosaurus was small compared to most members of its family and had a much shorter neck and larger head. Its name means "forked lizard" and comes from the forked spines that stuck out from its vertebrae. These may have helped to strengthen the backbone.

Mamenchisaurus

Mamenchisaurus had the longest neck of any animal known. It made up about half of the animal's total length and contained 19 extra-long vertebrae. Its long neck probably helped *Mamenchisaurus* reach fresh plant growth at the tops of trees.

Amargasaurus

Amargasaurus

This small diplodocid had two rows of spines growing up from its backbone. These may have helped to protect the dinosaur from predators. Or they may have been covered with skin to make a sail-like structure to help the dinosaur absorb or lose heat.

Apatosaurus

Although *Apatosaurus* would have moved on all fours, it may have been able to rear up on its back legs and bring its forelegs down to crush an enemy. Marks on the bones show that large muscles powered the tail, allowing the dinosaur to lash it from side to side to warn off attackers.

Seismosaurus

The remains of this sauropod, possibly the longest land animal ever, were first found by accident by two hikers in New Mexico. Its legs were short and thick to help support and steady its huge body, which may have weighed as much as 110 tons.

Seismosaurus

Apatosaurus

Sauropods

The first sauropods lived in the Early Jurassic. They reached their peak in the Late Jurassic and became extinct with the rest of the dinosaurs at the end of the Cretaceous. All had a similar body shape, with a long neck, massive body, and thick, heavy legs. In order to reduce the enormous weight of these gigantic plant eaters, the vertebrae (the bones that make up the backbone) were partly hollow, making them light for their size. In the earliest sauropods, such as cetiosaurs, the bones were only partly hollow, but in later types, such as diplodocids, the vertebrae became like bony struts, strong, but light. Diplodocids, therefore, weighed far less than bulky brachiosaurs and camarasaurs.

Plant eater

Like all sauropods, *Diplodocus* was a plant eater. Its small, closely packed teeth would have been just the right shape for stripping leaves from plants, but not for chewing. Smooth pebbles found near the fossils for these dinosaurs suggest that they may have swallowed stones to help to grind the food in their stomachs. Birds and crocodiles today swallow stones and grit for the same purpose.

Diplodocus

The head of *Diplodocus* was small for such a gigantic animal. Its neck was about 23 ft. (7 m) long and contained 15 vertebrae.

Early sauropod

Barapasaurus was a relative of the cetiosaurs, one of the earliest types of sauropod. Like its later relatives, it had a huge body and long neck and tail, but only some of its vertebrae were hollow so it would have been a very heavy animal.

Barapasaurus

Titanosaurs

The titanosaurs were the last type of sauropods to evolve. This group included dinosaurs such as *Saltasaurus* and *Alamosaurus*, which survived right up to the end of the Cretaceous. Less is known about this group since no complete skeletons have been found, but scientists think they ranged in size from 23 ft. (7 m) to a gigantic 82 or 100 ft. (25 or 30 m). Unlike other sauropods, they seem to have had bony plates covering their backs.

The special structure of the vertebrae (the bones making up the backbone) made *Diplodocus* amazingly light for its size. The vertebrae are partly hollow, some reduced to struts, so they weigh much less than if they were made of solid bone.

The legs of this dinosaur were like huge pillars supporting the body. The front feet were broad and had five toes. The first toe may have had a large claw, and the other toes ended in hooflike pads. The back feet had claws on the first and second toes. These claws could have been used to defend itself against attackers.

91

Boneheads and other Plant Eaters

Bonehead dinosaurs may have lived in herds much like the mountain goats of today. Like goats, they fed on plants and led peaceful lives for much of the time, but males probably fought fierce battles with rivals in the mating season. Much of the impact of their head-butting contests was taken by the tough bony dome on the head. Most bonehead fossils date from the Late Cretaceous and have been found in North America and central Asia. Like boneheads, fabrosaurs and heterodontosaurs were plant-eating dinosaurs and moved upright on long, slender legs.

Pisanosaurus

(T) Late Triassic

Size: 3 ft. (90 cm) long
Order: Ornithischia
Family: Pisanosauridae
Range: South America: Argentina
Pn: pee-SAN-oh-SAW-rus

Heterodontosaurus

Although similar to the fabrosaurs in appearance, *Heterodontosaurus* had quite different teeth. Unlike most other reptiles, it had three kinds—small pointed teeth like a mammal's incisors, which it used for nipping off leaves, larger back teeth for chewing, and two pairs of large canine teeth.

Heterodontosaurus

(J) Early Jurassic

Size: 3¼ ft. (1 m) long
Order: Ornithischia
Family: Heterodontosauridae
Range: southern Africa
Pn: HET-er-oh-DONT-oh-SAW-rus

Lesothosaurus

Small and lizardlike, this fabrosaur had long legs, short arms, and a slender tail. It moved upright on its back legs and could probably speed across the African plains to escape from enemies. As a plant eater, it had sharp, pointed teeth, shaped like little arrowheads, which it used to chop tough leaves.

(J) Early Jurassic

Size: 3 ft. (90 cm) long
Order: Ornithischia
Family: Fabrosauridae
Range: southern Africa
Pn: less-OH-toe-SAW-rus

Lesothosaurus

(Cr) Late Cretaceous

Size: 13 ft. (4 m) long
Order: Ornithischia
Family: Pachycephalosauridae
Range: North America: Alberta
Pn: PAK-ee-KEF-a-loh-SAW-rus

Stegoceras

Pisanosaurus

Few fossils have been found of this little dinosaur, but it may be one of the earliest of the ornithischian, or bird-hipped, dinosaurs. It lived during the Late Triassic period, millions of years before the other ornithischians appeared. It seems to have been lightly built and probably moved fast on its two back legs.

Pachycephalosaurus

The largest of the boneheads, this dinosaur had a huge dome on the top of its head made of solid bone, up to 10 in. (25 cm) thick. This dome probably acted like a crash helmet to protect the dinosaur's head when it took part in battles with rival males. The domes of males seem to have grown larger with age.

Pachycephalosaurus

Stegoceras

The thickened skull of *Stegoceras* was covered with lumps and knobs. When two males began a head-butting battle, they kept their heads lowered and neck, body and tail held straight out. The tail would have helped to balance the weight of the head.

Cr **Late Cretaceous**

Size: 6½ ft. (2 m) long
Order: Ornithischia
Family: Pachycephalosauridae
Range: North America: Alberta
Pn: steg-O-ser-as

Prenocephale

Like other boneheads, *Prenocephale* was a plant eater and probably fed on leaves and fruit. It walked on two legs and had five-fingered hands, three-toed feet, and a long heavy tail. The large dome on its head was surrounded with a row of bony spikes and bumps.

Cr **Late Cretaceous**

Size: 8 ft. (2.5 m) long
Order: Ornithischia
Family: Pachycephalosauridae
Range: Asia: Mongolia
Pn: pren-oh-KEF-a-lee

Prenocephale

Cr **Late Cretaceous**

Size: 10 ft. (3 m) long
Order: Ornithischia
Family: Homacephalidae
Range: Asia: Mongolia
Pn: home-ah-loh-KEF-ah-lee

Homalocephale

The homalocephalid family of boneheads did not have large domes on their heads. But the bones of the skull were heavy and thickened and the head was covered with bony knobs. *Homalocephale* also had unusually broad hips and some paleontologists believe that these took some of the impact when rival males fought.

Homalocephale

93

Hypsilophodonts

Hypsilophodonts were fast-running plant eaters, which
probably lived in herds like
deer today. When
danger threatened, they could have
escaped at high speed, running upright on their long,
slender back legs. A highly successful group,
hypsilophodonts lived from the Late Jurassic to the end of
the Cretaceous. Fossils have been found so far in North
America, Europe, Asia, Antarctica, and Australia. All
members of the family had tall, grooved cheek teeth for
grinding up plant food.

Parksosaurus

Size: 8 ft. (2.5 m) long
Order: Ornithischia
Family: Hypsilophodontidae
Range: North America: Alberta
Pn: PARX-oh-SAW-rus

Hypsilophodon

At one time scientists
believed that this dinosaur
may have lived in trees—
its body shape was
thought to be similar to
that of today's tree kangaroos.
However, further study has shown
that its feet are not suitable for
grasping trees and that this animal
was perfectly adapted for fast
movement on land.

Hypsilophodon

Early
Cretaceous

Size: 5 ft. (1.5 m) long
Order: Ornithischia
Family: Hypsilophodontidae
Range: North America: South
Dakota; Europe: England, Portugal
Pn: hip-see-LOAF-oh-don

Parksosaurus

Parksosaurus was one of the last
of the hypsilophodonts, surviving
until the end of the Cretaceous.
Although similar to its relatives, it
had bigger eyes than most and had
special bones to support its large
eyeballs. *Parksosaurus* probably fed
close to the ground, nipping off
leaves with its narrow beaked jaws.

Dryosaurus

Late
Jurassic   Early
Cretaceous

Size: 10 ft. (3 m) long
Order: Ornithischia
Range: western North America;
Africa; Europe: England, Romania;
possibly Australia
Pn: DRY-oh-SAW-rus

Dryosaurus

One of the largest of the
hypsilophodonts, *Dryosaurus* was
also one of the earliest. Like other
members of its family, it had long
legs that were built for speed, with
shin bones that were much longer
than its thigh bones. There were
three toes on each of its
slender feet.

Leaellynasaura

Fossils of this dinosaur were found in 1987 in the south of Australia. This region was once part of polar Gondwana, so the dinosaur must have been adapted to survive the long dark winters and freezing temperatures. Its eye sockets and the part of its brain devoted to vision were unusually large, suggesting that it had excellent sight.

Leaellynasaura

Cr Early Cretaceous

Size: 6½–10 ft. (2–3 m) long
Order: Ornithischia
Family: Hypsilophodontidae
Range: Australia
Pn: LEE-el-in-a-SAW-ra

Thescelosaurus

Bulkier than most of its relatives, *Thescelosaurus* also had teeth in the front of its upper jaw. The structure of its legs, with shin bones and thigh bones of the same length, suggest that it was slower moving than other hypsilophodonts. But it did have rows of bony studs on its back that may have helped to protect it from enemies.

Othnielia

Othnielia

A typical hypsilophodont, *Othnielia* had long legs, a lightweight body, and short arms with five-fingered hands. Originally known as *Nanosaurus*, it was renamed in honor of the 19th-century American fossil collector Professor Othniel Charles Marsh to commemorate his work on dinosaurs.

J Late Jurassic

Size: 4½ ft. (1.4 m) long
Order: Ornithischia
Family: Hypsilophodontidae
Range: North America: Utah, Wyoming
Pn: oth-ni-EL-ee-a

Cr Late Cretaceous

Size: 11½ ft. (3.5 m) long
Order: Ornithischia
Family: Hypsilophodontidae
Range: North America: Alberta, Montana, Saskatchewan, Wyoming
Pn: thes-KEL-oh-SAW-rus

Thescelosaurus

Tenontosaurus

Tenontosaurus was much bulkier than most of its family and over half its length was made up of its heavy tail. It probably spent much of its time on all fours and it had longer arms than other hypsilophodonts. Daggerlike claws on its feet would have helped it defend itself from enemies.

Cr Early Cretaceous

Size: 24 ft. (7.3 m) long
Order: Ornithischia
Family: Hypsilophodontidae
Range: North America: Arizona, Montana, Oklahoma, Texas
Pn: teh-NON-toe-SAW-rus

Tenontosaurus

95

Iguanodonts

Large plant-eating dinosaurs, iguanodonts appeared in the Jurassic and spread all over the world. They were bulky, big-boned animals with sturdy legs and hooflike nails on their feet. Each short arm had a five-fingered hand, which could be spread wide and used for walking when on all fours. Instead of a thumb, each hand bore a sharp spike. Probably fairly slow-moving, iguanodonts would have spent most of their time on all fours browsing on low-growing plants. They could also rear up on to their hind legs to reach leaves higher in the trees.

Vectisaurus

Vectisaurus

A close relative of *Iguanodon*, *Vectisaurus* lived at the same time and in the same area. The only difference between the two, apart from size, was that *Vectisaurus* had spines growing upward from its backbone that were long enough to form a definite ridge along the back.

Cr Early Cretaceous

Size: 13 ft. (4 m) long
Order: Ornithischia
Family: Iguanodontidae
Range: Europe: England
Pn: VECK-ti-SAW-rus

Muttaburrasaurus

Found in Australia in 1981, fossils of this iguanodont show that it had a bony bump on its skull just in front of the eyes. No one knows exactly what this was used for, but it could have been used in displays to attract mates.

Cr Early Cretaceous

Size: 24 ft. (7.3 m) long
Order: Ornithischia
Family: Iguanodontidae
Range: Australia: Queensland
Pn: MUT-a-BUR-a-SAW-rus

Muttaburrasaurus

Ouranosaurus

Ouranosaurus had a row of spines running down the center of its back. These spines would have been covered with skin to form a finlike structure that may have helped the dinosaur control its temperature—when the fin was turned to the sun it would have absorbed heat.

Cr Early Cretaceous

Size: 23 ft. (7 m) long
Order: Ornithischia
Family: Iguanodontidae
Range: Africa: Nigeria
Pn: OO-ran-oh-SAW-rus

Ouranosaurus

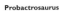

Iguanodon

Iguanodon was the second dinosaur to be discovered—part of a leg bone was found in 1809 in southern England. Fossilized footprints suggest that *Iguanodon* lived in herds and was probably slow moving. It would have spent most of its time on four legs, but could have reared up on two to feed on plants higher up.

Cr Early Cretaceous

Size: 30 ft. (9 m) long
Order: Ornithischia
Family: Iguanodontidae
Range: Europe: Belgium, England, Germany; North America: Utah; Africa: Tunisia; Asia: Mongolia
Pn: ig-WA-no-don

Probactrosaurus

Like all iguanodonts, *Probactrosaurus* had a strong toothless beak for chopping mouthfuls of plant food. Farther back in the jaws were ridged teeth for grinding food down. New teeth grew as old ones wore out.

Cr Early Cretaceous

Size: 20 ft. (6 m) long
Order: Ornithischia
Family: Iguanodontidae
Range: Asia: China
Pn: pro-BAK-troh-SAW-rus

Camptosaurus

An early member of the iguanodont family, *Camptosaurus* had four toes on each foot (other iguanodonts had three) and a poorly developed thumb spike. Like the rest of its family, this dinosaur had small hooves on its fingers and toes.

Camptosaurus

J Late Jurassic

Size: 20 ft. (6 m) long
Order: Ornithischia
Family: Iguanodontidae
Range: Europe: England, Portugal; North America
Pn: KAMP-toe-SAW-rus

Rhabdodon

When standing upright on their back legs, iguanodonts such as *Rhabdodon* would have held the long tail straight out behind to help balance the heavy weight of the body. This iguanodont lived on a group of volcanic islands located where central Europe is now.

Rhabdodon

Cr Early Cretaceous

Size: 13 ft. (4 m) long
Order: Ornithischia
Family: Iguanodontidae
Range: Europe: France, Romania
Pn: RAB-doh-don

Iguanodonts

Iguanodonts are named after the best known member of their family—*Iguanodon*. Gideon Mantell, the 19th century fossil hunter who first discovered the dinosaur's remains, realized that its teeth were similar to those of a modern iguana lizard. So he gave it the name *Iguanodon* or "iguana tooth." In this scene in Cretaceous Europe, *Iguanodon* and other plant eaters browse on horsetails while watching out for an approaching predator—*Megalosaurus*.

Thumb spike

On each hand *Iguanodon* had a sharp spike instead of a thumb. The dinosaur may have used this to defend itself against its enemies, jabbing the spike into the eye or neck of an attacker. Three of the other fingers were like pointed hooves, and *Iguanodon* walked on these when it moved on all fours. The other finger was very flexible and could be bent across the palm and used to hold onto food. In the first reconstructions of *Iguanodon*, scientists mistook the spike for a horn and placed it on the dinosaur's nose!

Megalosaurus

Polacanthus

Bernissartia

Hypsilophodon

Feeding

Iguanodon had no teeth at the front of its jaws, but had a turtlelike beak, ideal for chopping off mouthfuls of tough leaves. Farther back in its jaws were strong teeth for chewing its food. New teeth developed as old ones wore out. To reach juicy leaves high in the trees, *Iguanodon* could rear up on its two back legs. Its strong tail acted as a prop to help support it as it fed. When the dinosaur walked on two legs, the tail helped to balance the weight of the front of its body.

Ouranosaurus

Muttaburrasaurus

Toothless beaks

All iguanodonts had toothless beaks made of a hornlike material, but these varied in size and shape. *Ouranosaurus*, an African iguanodont, had a wide, flat snout and a large beak. The Australian *Muttaburrasaurus* had a smaller head and slender beak. Both had bony bumps on the skull.

Iguanodon

Baryonyx

Horsetail

99

Duckbilled Dinosaurs

Also known as hadrosaurs, duckbilled dinosaurs get their name from their long, flattened beak. One of the largest and most varied of Late Cretaceous dinosaur groups, hadrosaurs were particularly common in North America and Asia. All had long back legs and shorter front legs. They probably spent much of their time on all fours while feeding but could rear up on their back legs to run away from attackers. They are thought to have lived in herds and nested in groups. Although some hadrosaurs had flat heads, many had a strangely shaped crest on the top of the head.

Edmontosaurus

Like all hadrosaurs, *Edmontosaurus* had a toothless beak for cropping plants. Behind this, in both upper and lower jaws, were as many as a thousand tightly packed teeth for grinding down the food. As teeth became worn they were replaced with new ones. The neck was strong yet bendy, allowing the dinosaur to gather low-growing plants from a wide area around it, without having to move.

Anatosaurus

Anatosaurus

Two "mummified" bodies of *Anatosaurus* dinosaurs have provided rare clues to their diet. The stomach contents include pine needles, twigs, seeds, and fruit. Like other hadrosaurs, it may have stood up on its back legs to gather food from trees.

> **Cr** Late Cretaceous
>
> **Size:** 33 ft. (10 m) long
> **Order:** Ornithischia
> **Family:** Hadrosauridae
> **Range:** North America: Alberta
> **Pn:** an-at-oh-SAW-rus

Shantungosaurus

One of the biggest hadrosaurs known, *Shantungosaurus* had a particularly long tail, measuring up to almost half the total body length. Deep and flattened in shape, the tail was held out behind to help balance the body weight when the dinosaur walked upright. *Shantungosaurus* may have weighed as much as 5 tons.

Bactrosaurus

Bactrosaurus

This is the earliest known duckbilled dinosaur. The group appeared in the Late Cretaceous at the same time as flowering plants spread throughout the world. This plentiful food supply—and their efficient plant-grinding jaws for making use of it—may have been the reason for the great success of the duckbills.

> **Cr** Late Cretaceous
>
> **Size:** 13 ft. (4 m) long
> **Order:** Ornithischia
> **Family:** Hadrosauridae
> **Range:** Asia: Mongolia and China
> **Pn:** bak-troh-SAW-rus

> **Cr** Late Cretaceous
>
> **Size:** 43 ft. (13 m) long
> **Order:** Ornithischia
> **Family:** Hadrosauridae
> **Range:** Asia: China
> **Pn:** shan-TUNG-oh-SAW-rus

Edmontosaurus

Hadrosaurus

Cr Early
Cretaceous

Size: 30 ft. (9 m) long
Order: Ornithischia
Family: Hadrosauridae
Range: North America: Montana,
New Jersey, New Mexico, South
Dakota
Pn: HAD-roh-SAW-rus

Hadrosaurus

This duckbill was the first
dinosaur to be discovered in
North America. Its bones were
found in New Jersey and it was
reconstructed and named in 1858.
Like *Kritosaurus*, *Hadrosaurus* was
a flat-headed duckbill. It had no
crest but there was a large hump
made of bone on its snout.

Cr Late
Cretaceous

Size: 43 ft. (13 m) long
Order: Ornithischia
Family: Hadrosauridae
Range: North America: Alberta,
Montana
Pn: ed-MON-toh-SAW-rus

Kritosaurus

No one knows exactly why
flat-headed dinosaurs such as
Kritosaurus had bony humps on
their snouts. It is possible that
only the males had humps and
that they used them in courtship
displays.

Maiasaura

Maiasaura

The discovery of a complete
Maiasaura nest site in Montana
proved that dinosaurs were
social animals. The females
nested in groups and may even
have returned to the same site
year after year like turtles and
many birds today. It is possible
that the dinosaurs also shared
the care of the young, some
remaining on guard while
others fed.

Cr Late
Cretaceous

Size: 30 ft. (9 m) long
Order: Ornithischia
Family: Hadrosauridae
Range: North America: Montana
Pn: my-ah-SAW-rah

Kritosaurus

Shantungosaurus

Cr Late
Cretaceous

Size: 30 ft. (9 m) long
Order: Ornithischia
Family: Hadrosauridae
Range: North America: Alberta,
Montana, New Mexico
Pn: KRITE-oh-SAW-rus

Protohadros

Protohadros

Discovered in Texas, which would have been covered with marshland at the time, *Protohadros* is the oldest, most primitive duckbill known. The fact that it was found in the United States means that duckbills may not have first evolved in Asia as scientists previously believed.

(Cr) Late Cretaceous

Size: up to 20 ft. (6 m) long
Order: Ornithischia
Family: Hadrosauridae
Range: North America: Texas
Pn: pro-toe-HAD-ross

Saurolophus

The face of this duckbill curved upward from its broad snout to the tip of the bony crest on the top of the head. A fleshy nose sac, which helped make the dinosaur's calls louder, may have been attached to the crest.

Saurolophus

(Cr) Late Cretaceous

Size: 30 ft. (9 m) long
Order: Ornithischia
Family: Hadrosauridae
Range: North America: Alberta; California; Asia: Mongolia
Pn: SORE-oh-LOAF-us

Parasaurolophus

(Cr) Late Cretaceous

Size: 30 ft. (9 m) long
Order: Ornithischia
Family: Hadrosauridae
Range: North America: Alberta, New Mexico, Utah
Pn: par-a-SORE-oh-LOAF-us

Parasaurolophus

A spectacular, backward-pointing crest, more than 6 ft. (1.8 m) long, topped the head of this dinosaur. The crest was hollow inside and may have acted like an echo chamber to make the dinosaur's booming calls louder. When the dinosaur held its head up, the crest may have fitted into a small notch in the backbone.

Tsintaosaurus

A tall horn grew from the top of this duckbill's head. It pointed straight up from between the eyes and had a notched tip. There has been much disagreement among experts about the position and use of this horn. Some think there may have been a flap of skin attached that was used like a flag for signalling to other members of the herd or in courtship rituals.

Prosaurolophus

Corythosaurus

A spectacular fan-shaped crest crowned the head of this duckbill. Crests of several different sizes have been found. Smaller crests may have belonged to young animals or females.

Cr Late Cretaceous

Size: 26 ft. (8 m) long
Order: Ornithischia
Family: Hadrosauridae
Range: North America: Alberta
Pn: PRO-sore-oh-LOAF-us

Corythosaurus

Cr Late Cretaceous

Size: 30 ft. (9 m) long
Order: Ornithischia
Family: Hadrosauridae
Range: North America: Alberta, Montana
Pn: ko-RITH-oh-SAW-rus

Prosaurolophus

This duckbill had a low crest of bone running from the tip of the flat snout up to the top of the head. It ended in a small bony knob. Like all duckbills, *Prosaurolophus* had a toothless beak at the front of its head for gathering plant food.

Lambeosaurus

Lambeosaurus

Like all members of its family, *Lambeosaurus* would have moved about on all fours as it fed. But if threatened, it could probably rear up on its back legs to run away. It had two structures on its head—a tall hollow crest at the front and a solid bony spike pointing backward.

Cr Late Cretaceous

Size: 30 ft. (9 m) long
Order: Ornithischia
Family: Hadrosauridae
Range: North America: Baja California, Montana, Saskatchewan
Pn: LAM-bee-oh-SAW-rus

Hypacrosaurus

Hypacrosaurus had a semicircular crest on its head similar to that of *Corythosaurus*. This duckbill also had tall spines along its back— these probably formed a skin-covered ridge. The ridge may have helped it control its body temperature— when turned to the sun the ridge could absorb heat.

Cr Late Cretaceous

Size: 30 ft. (9 m) long
Order: Ornithischia
Family: Hadrosauridae
Range: North America: Alberta, Montana
Pn: hie-PAK-roe-SAW-rus

Tsintaosaurus

Cr Late Cretaceous

Size: 33 ft. (10 m) long
Order: Ornithischia
Family: Hadrosauridae
Range: Asia: China
Pn: SIN-tow-SAW-rus

Hypacrosaurus

Stegosaurs

Scutellosaurus

Stegosaurs were large, plant-eating dinosaurs. A typical stegosaur had a small head, huge body, and heavy tail, lined with long sharp spikes. The most extraordinary features of these dinosaurs were the rows of large triangular plates on the back. There are several different ideas about their use, but many experts believe that they helped to control body temperature. The plates may have been covered with skin rich in blood vessels. When the stegosaur turned toward the sun, its blood would have been warmed as it passed through the plates. When the animal turned away from the sun or into a breeze, the plates would have lost heat, cooling the body.

Scutellosaurus

This dinosaur was an early form of stegosaur. Lining its back and sides were rows of bony studs that may have helped to protect the animal from attackers. Its tail was about half its total length and could have been held out to balance the weight of the body when the dinosaur ran on two legs.

(J) Late Jurassic

Size: 23 ft. (7 m) long
Order: Ornithischia
Family: Stegosauridae
Range: Asia: China
Pn: toh-HWANG-oh-SAW-rus

Tuojiangosaurus

This Chinese stegosaur had a small narrow head and a heavy body. Its back was lined with 15 pairs of bony plates, which were taller and spikier toward the hips. The long spikes on the tail could have been used as a weapon against attackers. *Tuojiangosaurus* was the first stegosaur to be found in Asia.

Tuojiangosaurus

Wuerhosaurus

Only a few bones and plates have been found belonging to this dinosaur so no one knows exactly how it looked. *Wuerhosaurus* was one of the few stegosaurs to have survived into the Early Cretaceous—the group began to die out toward the end of the Jurassic period.

(Cr) Early Cretaceous

Size: 20 ft. (6 m) long
Order: Ornithischia
Family: Stegosauridae
Range: Asia: China
Pn: WER-oh-SAW-us

Wuerhosaurus

Stegosaurus

One of the largest and best known stegosaurs, *Stegosaurus* had a double row of bony plates on its back, some measuring up to 24 in. (60 cm) high. The heavy tail was armed with spikes up to 3¼ ft. (1 m) long.

J Early Jurassic

Size: 4 ft. (1.2 m) long
Order: Ornithischia
Family: Scelidosauridae
Range: North America: Arizona
Pn: skoot-EL-oh-SAW-rus

Lexovisaurus

Some experts believe that the bony plates on stegosaurs were not used for controlling body temperature but for helping the dinosaurs recognize their own species and attract mates. The arrangement of plates and spines was different in each species. *Lexovisaurus* had two rows of large thin plates.

J Middle Jurassic

Size: 16 ft. (5 m) long
Order: Ornithischia
Family: Stegosauridae
Range: Europe: England
Pn: lex-OH-vi-SAW-rus

Scelidosaurus

J Early Jurassic

Size: 13 ft. (4 m) long
Order: Ornithischia
Family: Scelidosauridae
Range: Europe: England
Pn: skel-ID-oh-SAW-rus

Lexovisaurus

Scelidosaurus

One of the earliest ornithischian dinosaurs, *Scelidosaurus* may have been an early form of stegosaur. It had a small head, a toothless beak, and little teeth that were set farther back in its jaws. Its heavy body was covered in bony plates, studded with rows of spikes running from the neck to the tail.

Kentrosaurus

J Late Jurassic

Size: 16 ft. (5 m) long
Order: Ornithischia
Family: Stegosauridae
Range: Africa: Tanzania
Pn: KEN-tro-SAW-rus

Stegosaurus

J Late Jurassic

Size: 30 ft. (9 m) long
Order: Ornithischia
Family: Stegosauridae
Range: North America: Colorado, Oklahoma, Utah, Wyoming
Pn: STEG-oh-SAW-rus

Kentrosaurus

Smaller than *Stegosaurus*, *Kentrosaurus* was almost as well armored with bony plates and spikes. If attacked, the stegosaur could lash out with its spiked tail and wound its attacker. Long spikes at hip level provided extra protection against enemies.

Stegosaurus

The biggest of the stegosaurs, *Stegosaurus* had rows of huge bony plates shaped like arrowheads all along its back. These may have helped the animal control its body temperature (see page 104), but would have also made it more difficult for a predator to attack. Some scientists now think that the plates may have played a part in courtship. They were rich in blood vessels and could have flushed deep red when the stegosaur wanted to attract a mate.

Bony plates

No stegosaur has been found with the bony plates still attached to the skeleton. Experts once thought they were arranged in pairs. Now most agree that they were arranged in two alternating rows as shown here.

Stegosaurus skeleton

The back legs of *Stegosaurus* were more than twice as long as the front legs, making the body slope forward from the hips. The large, bony plates on the back were as much as 24 in. (60 cm) tall, while the head of *Stegosaurus* was small for its body size—the skull measured only about 16 in. (40 cm) long. At the front of the jaws was a toothless beak, and farther back were some small teeth.

Defense

Stegosaurs were probably not fast movers and could not sprint on two legs to escape from enemies. Instead, a stegosaur probably stood its ground when threatened and lashed out at its attacker with its heavy spiked tail. Each spike may have been as much as a yard long. The dinosaur may have been able to twist its body around surprisingly quick, and a blow from this tail could cause severe damage to the legs of a predator. *Stegosaurus* was longer than a present day African elephant and probably weighed more than 2 tons. Such an animal did not make an easy meal for any predator.

Feeding

Stegosaurus probably spent most of its time on four legs, but may have reared up on its two back legs to reach leaves on tall trees, as shown here.

The broad three-toed back feet helped to spread the stegosaur's massive weight. On the front feet were five clawed toes.

The long spikes at the end of the tail may have been covered with tough horn, like the horns of cattle today.

107

Family Life

Like reptiles and birds today, most dinosaurs would have laid hard-shelled eggs in which their young grew. Although many fossil eggs have been found, few can be definitely identified as belonging to a particular species. Those that can be identified show that some dinosaurs looked after their eggs and young. In a nest belonging to *Troodon*, for example, eggs were arranged in a circle with the tips pointing neatly in toward the center. The nest also had a built-up rim surrounding it. One fossilized *Oviraptor* was found incubating its clutch.

The egg

A duckbilled dinosaur's egg was about 7 in. (18 cm) long and had a tough, waterproof shell to protect the growing baby inside. A newly hatched *Maiasaura* probably measured about 12 in. (30 cm). Fossils of leg bones show that the baby duckbill would have been too weak to move far and would have stayed in the nest for a few weeks being fed by its parents.

A caring mother

Fossilized eggs belonging to the duckbilled dinosaur *Maiasaura* (see page 101) were discovered arranged in circles in the middle of a nest mound. The mother probably lay next to the nest to guard her eggs from predators. Other remains of lots of little *Maiasaura* dinosaurs, all about the same age, show that the young were probably cared for in groups by a few adults while others went off to find food.

Battling boneheads

Dinosaurs such as boneheads (see pages 92–93) probably lived in herds. In the breeding season male boneheads may have fought fierce head-butting battles to win females or the leadership of the group. Some herding animals, such as mountain goats, do the same today.

This clutch of **fossilized eggs** belonging to *Oviraptor* was discovered in the Gobi Desert, Mongolia. Several such clutches have been found, some containing as many as 22 eggs.

Keeping in touch

Fossilized tracks and finds of groups of bones show that many types of plant-eating dinosaurs lived in herds. Like plant eaters today, they would have found that moving in herds helped to protect them from predators. Duckbilled dinosaurs, or hadrosaurs, may have made special calls to keep in touch with others in their herd, as well as to attract mates. The differently shaped crests on the duckbills may have acted as echo chambers to help make the calls louder. The crests may also have helped the dinosaurs recognize others of their own species. Females may have had smaller crests than males.

Lambeosaurus

Corythosaurus

Parasaurolophus

Hypacrosaurus

Duckbilled dinosaur crests

Living in a Herd

It is impossible to be sure how dinosaurs lived, but evidence such as fossilized footprints do provide valuable clues. Groups of footprints have been discovered, for example, that suggest that dinosaurs moved in herds, just like many plant-eating animals today. Smaller footprints in among the big ones may have belonged to young dinosaurs, moving at the center of the herd for protection from predators. Discoveries of large numbers of skeletons together are also evidence that some types of dinosaurs, such as duckbills and horned dinosaurs, lived in herds.

Fossilized footprints

Long ago, a herd of sauropod dinosaurs would come to rivers to drink, leaving their footprints in the mud. Long dry spells would follow, and the footprints were baked hard. Even though they were later covered by more mud, the prints remained. Millions of years later, as the surface of the land is eroded the footprints are once again revealed, telling their story about the lives of dinosaurs.

Herd of sauropod dinosaurs

Fossilized footprints or trackways also provide information about how dinosaurs moved. From footprints, experts can tell whether a dinosaur ran on four legs or two, how wide its body was and even how fast it was traveling.

Parents and young

Young dinosaurs, even the young of giant sauropods such as *Camarasaurus*, would have been very vulnerable to attack by predators. For safety the young would have stayed near their parents and moved at the center of the herd. The evidence from fossil bones of young sauropods shows that they grew very quickly and may have gained as much as 7 lb (3 kg) a day.

Camarasaurus

Horned dinosaurs such as *Triceratops* are thought to have lived in herds. Just like herds of musk oxen today, they may have defended their young against attack by forming a circle around them and threatening the predator with their mighty horned heads.

111

Cretaceous Times

Pteranodon, a flying reptile (pterosaur)

The biggest change that took place during the Cretaceous period, which began 146 million years ago, was the appearance of the first flowering plants. Small herbs, bushes, and deciduous trees took over from horsetails and cycads, and became the dominant greenery on the Earth. There was more plant food than ever, allowing huge herds of plant eaters, such as horned dinosaurs and duckbills, to thrive. With flowering plants came pollinating insects and many more species of mammals and birds.

Cretaceous North America

In this scene in what is now Montana, a duckbill dinosaur bellows her alarm as she returns to her nest to find an agile *Troodon* stealing her eggs. Lizards and an early mammal scuttle by, while a tyrannosaur stalks nearer to a group of feeding horned dinosaurs.

Magnolia

Sycamore

Albertosaurus, a tyrannosaur

Small mammal

Centrosaurus, a horned dinosaur

Lizard

Moss

Troodon

The Cretaceous world

In the Cretaceous period, the world's landmasses continued to drift apart until by the end of the period they were close to their positions today. The climate was generally warm and there were greater differences between the seasons. As the land broke into smaller pieces, greater differences between the dinosaurs in different continents developed as they evolved in isolation from each other.

Montana — North America

Europe

Asia

ATLANTIC OCEAN

Turkey

PACIFIC OCEAN

South America

Africa

TETHYS OCEAN

India

Australia

Antarctica

Key to map

☐ Ocean

☐ Landmass

☐ Sea-covered continent

Corythosaurus

Conifer

Early oystercatcher

Troodon, a bird relative (maniraptoran)

Corythosaurus, a duckbilled dinosaur

Lizard

113

Cretaceous America

There were more kinds of dinosaur in the late Cretaceous than at any other time. In this North American forest, a mighty *Tyrannosaurus* thunders into view, scattering a herd of plant-eating *Corythosaurus* and a *Parasaurolophus*. Also fleeing from the predator is *Alphadon*, an early species of marsupial, or pouched mammal. Flowering plants were starting to grow in the forests of North America at this time.

Parasaurolophus

Alphadon

Tyrannosaurus

Corythosaurus

Panoplosaurus

Armored Dinosaurs

Two groups of heavily armored dinosaurs were common in the Cretaceous period—nodosaurs and ankylosaurs. In both, the neck, back, sides, and tail were covered with flat plates of bone, set into the thick leathery skin. Nodosaurs had narrow skulls and long spikes that stuck out at the sides of the body. Ankylosaurs had broader skulls and a heavy ball of bone like a club at the end of the tail. If attacked, an ankylosaur could swing this from side to side and cause severe damage to its attacker. The broad-snouted ankylosaurs probably ate any low plants they could find, whereas the nodosaurs, with their narrower muzzles, may have selected certain leaves.

Cr Late Cretaceous

Size: 15 ft. (4.5 m) long
Order: Ornithischia
Family: Nodosauridae
Range: North America: Alberta, Montana, South Dakota, Texas
Pn: pan-o-ploe-SAW-rus

Panoplosaurus

This heavily armored nodosaur had broad plates of bone across its neck and shoulders while the rest of the back was covered in smaller bony studs. Huge spikes guarded each side and even the head was protected with thick pieces of bone.

Euoplocephalus

Hylaeosaurus

Cr Late Cretaceous

Size: 18 ft. (5.5 m) long
Order: Ornithischia
Family: Ankylosauridae
Range: North America: Alberta
Pn: you-op-loh-KEF-ah-lus

Euoplocephalus

Like other ankylosaurs, this dinosaur had a heavy bony club at the end of its tail that could have weighed more than 60 lb (27 kg). Powerful muscles at the hips helped *Euoplocephalus* swing its clubbed tail from side to side against any attacker.

Cr Early Cretaceous

Size: 20 ft. (6 m) long
Order: Ornithischia
Family: Nodosauridae
Range: Europe: England
Pn: hy-lee-oh-SAW-rus

Hylaeosaurus

Hylaeosaurus was one of the earliest dinosaurs to be described and named. A fossil was found in southern England in the 1820s by Gideon Mantell, one of the first ever dinosaur experts. The bones are still imprisoned in the block of limestone in which they were found but the creature is believed to be a nodosaur.

Saichania

Like most ankylosaurs, *Saichania* had a network of air passages inside its skull. These may have helped to cool or moisten air before it reached the dinosaur's lungs. This was important because Mongolia at this time was hot and humid, but with very dry spells.

Cr Late Cretaceous

Size: 23 ft. (7 m) long
Order: Ornithischia
Family: Ankylosauridae
Range: Asia: Mongolia
Pn: sy-KAHN-ee-a

Saichania

Talarurus

Cr Late Cretaceous

Size: 16 ft. (5 m) long
Order: Ornithischia
Family: Ankylosauridae
Range: Asia: Mongolia
Pn: tal-a-ROO-rus

Talarurus

Like all armored dinosaurs, *Talarurus* ate plants, which it cropped with the toothless beak at the front of its jaws. The club on the end of its tail was made from two large balls of bone joined together. Thin bony rods strengthened the tail to support the heavy club.

Sauropelta

This tanklike creature is the largest known nodosaur. It may have weighed as much as 3 tons. Bony, horn-covered plates protected its back, and sharp spikes stuck out from each side. Its bulk made *Sauropelta* slow moving, but its armor would have put off all but the most determined predators.

Cr Early Cretaceous

Size: 25 ft. (7.6 m) long
Order: Ornithischia
Family: Nodosauridae
Range: North America: Montana
Pn: SAW-roh-PEL-ta

Sauropelta

Polacanthus

Few fossils of this dinosaur have been found, but it is thought to have had large spines protecting its shoulders and tail. Smaller spiny plates guarded the sides and a mass of bone covered the hips. Like other nodosaurs, it may have crouched down when attacked, relying on its armor for defense.

Cr Early Cretaceous

Size: 13 ft. (4 m) long
Order: Ornithischia
Family: Nodosauridae
Range: Europe: England
Pn: pol-a-KAN-thus

Polacanthus

Horned Dinosaurs

There were three main groups of horned dinosaurs. First came the "parrot dinosaurs," or psittacosaurs, of the Early Cretaceous. These lightly built dinosaurs had distinctive parrotlike beaks. In the Late Cretaceous came the protoceratopids, which had heavier bodies and the beginnings of the bony neck frills that developed so dramatically in the later ceratopsians. The ceratopsians were the most common large plant eaters in Late Cretaceous western North America. These well-armored dinosaurs had long sharp horns on their massive heads and a bony frill at the back of the neck.

Bagaceratops

Bagaceratops

This little protoceratopid had a squat body and long tail, supported on four solid legs. At the back of its neck was a bony ridge and there was a short horn halfway along its snout. Unlike other members of its family, it had no teeth in its upper beak.

Cr Late Cretaceous

Size: 3¼ ft. (1 m) long
Order: Ornithischia
Family: Protoceratopidae
Range: Asia: Mongolia
Pn: BAG-a-SER-a-tops

Microceratops

Microceratops

The smallest horned dinosaur known, *Microceratops* was lightly built and was probably a fast runner. Its shin bones were almost twice as long as its thigh bones—a sign of a speedy dinosaur. It may have moved on all fours as it fed on plants, rising up on two legs to escape from danger.

Cr Late Cretaceous

Size: 24 in. (60 cm) long
Order: Ornithischia
Family: Protoceratopidae
Range: Asia: China, Mongolia
Pn: mik-roh-SERRA-tops

Psittacosaurus

A parrotlike toothless beak covered with horn is the reason for this dinosaur's name, which means "parrot lizard." This dinosaur fed on plants, which it cropped with its strong beak. It had bony ridges on the sides of its head but no neck frill like the later ceratopsians.

Psittacosaurus

Cr Early Cretaceous

Size: 8 ft. (2.5 m) long
Order: Ornithischia
Family: Psittacosauridae
Range: Asia: China, Mongolia, Siberia
Pn: si-TAK-oh-SAW-rus

Montanoceratops

Although it had a definite horn on its snout, *Montanoceratops* was a protoceratopid, not a member of the more advanced ceratopsian family. Its tail was unusually deep and flexible and could probably have been moved rapidly from side to side. The tail may have been used as a courtship signal in the mating season or as a way of recognizing its own species.

Leptoceratops

This was one of the few protoceratopids to be found in North America. Most of the family lived in Asia. Its back legs were built for running and it could probably move on four legs or two. The five-clawed fingers on its hands could have been used for picking leaves and passing them to the mouth.

Leptoceratops

Cr Late Cretaceous

Size: 7 ft. (2.1 m) long
Order: Ornithischia
Family: Protoceratopidae
Range: North America: Alberta, Wyoming; Asia: Mongolia
Pn: LEP-toe-SER-a-tops

Protoceratops

When fully grown this dinosaur probably weighed almost 400 lb (180 kg). An impressive creature, it had a large bony neck frill at the back of its heavy head and powerful beaked jaws. It had a large bump on its snout that may have been used in fights between rival males.

Protoceratops

Cr Late Cretaceous

Size: 9 ft. (2.7 m) long
Order: Ornithischia
Family: Protoceratopidae
Range: Asia: China, Mongolia
Pn: PRO-toe-SER-a-tops

Montanoceratops

Cr Late Cretaceous

Size: 10 ft. (3 m) long
Order: Ornithischia
Family: Protoceratopidae
Range: North America: Montana
Pn: mon-tan-oh-SERRA-tops

Chasmosaurus

This horned dinosaur had a huge bony neck frill that stretched from the back of the skull to cover its neck and shoulders. A spectacular frill like this could have been used to warn off enemies as well as to attract females.

Chasmosaurus

Late Cretaceous

Size: 17 ft. (5.2 m) long
Order: Ornithischia
Family: Ceratopsidae
Range: North America: Alberta
Pn: KAZ-mo-SAW-rus

Anchiceratops

This horned dinosaur lived near the end of the Late Cretaceous and was slightly more streamlined than some of its relatives. Its body was longer and its bony neck frill narrower. Like other horned dinosaurs, it fed on plants, which it gathered with its sharp, toothless beak.

Anchiceratops

Cr Late Cretaceous

Size: 20 ft. (6 m) long
Order: Ornithischia
Family: Ceratopsidae
Range: North America: Alberta
Pn: AN-ki-SER-a-tops

Cr Late Cretaceous

Size: 20 ft. (6 m) long
Order: Ornithischia
Family: Ceratopsidae
Range: North America: New Mexico
Pn: PEN-ta-SER-a-tops

Triceratops

One of the largest and most common horned dinosaurs, *Triceratops* weighed as much as 10 tons. Its skull alone was more than 6 ft. (1.8 m) long. Like others in its family, *Triceratops* probably lived in large herds. Rival males may have fought one another, locking horns and pushing with their head shields.

Pentaceratops

Pentaceratops

Like *Chasmosaurus*, this horned dinosaur had a huge neck frill, which was fringed with small spines. There were several large openings in the bony surface to make the frill lighter. The name of this dinosaur means "five-horned face" because scientists thought it had horns on its cheeks as well as on its snout. In fact, these were just elongated cheek bones.

Cr Late Cretaceous

Size: 30 ft. (9 m) long
Order: Ornithischia
Family: Ceratopsidae
Range: North America: Alberta, Colorado, Montana, Saskatchewan, South Dakota, Wyoming
Pn: try-SER-ah-tops

Triceratops

Torosaurus

Torosaurus

The skull of this dinosaur is one of the largest known of any land animal, living or extinct. Including the enormous neck frill, which extended from the back of the head, it measured more than 8 ft. (2.5 m). With this and the three pointed horns on its snout, *Torosaurus* was a challenge for any predator.

Cr Late Cretaceous

Size: 25 ft. (7.6 m) long
Order: Ornithischia
Family: Ceratopsidae
Range: North America: Montana, South Dakota, Texas, Utah, Wyoming
Pn: TOR-oh-SAW-rus

Pachyrhinosaurus

The skulls that have been found suggest that *Pachyrhinosaurus* had no horns on its snout. Instead, it had a thick bony pad just above the eyes. This may have protected the head, like the thickened skull of boneheads (see pages 92–93), or may simply have marked the place where the horns had fallen off.

Pachyrhinosaurus

Cr Late Cretaceous

Size: 18 ft. (5.5 m) long
Order: Ornithischia
Family: Ceratopsidae
Range: North America: Alberta
Pn: PAK-ee-RINE-oh-SAW-rus

Styracosaurus

Styracosaurus

The amazing bony neck frill of this horned dinosaur had an array of sharp spikes around the edge. With these and its great nose horn, *Styracosaurus* could have defended itself against attackers by charging toward them with head held down, just like a rhinoceros today.

Cr Late Cretaceous

Size: 17 ft. (5.2 m) long
Order: Ornithischia
Family: Ceratopsidae
Range: North America: Alberta, Montana
Pn: sty-RAK-oh-SAW-rus

Centrosaurus

Like other horned dinosaurs, *Centrosaurus* had thick pillarlike legs with heavy bones to support the bulky body. The short wide toes were fanned out to help spread the weight. Despite the size of its head and bony neck frill, a mobile neck joint ensured that *Centrosaurus* could turn its head quickly and easily.

Cr Late Cretaceous

Size: 20 ft. (6 m) long
Order: Ornithischia
Family: Ceratopsidae
Range: North America: Alberta, Montana
Pn: SEN-troh-SAW-rus

Centrosaurus

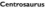

Triceratops

The largest and heaviest of all the horned
dinosaurs was *Triceratops*, which was twice the
length of a modern rhinoceros and weighed more
than an African elephant. Its name means "three-
horned face." *Triceratops* probably lived in herds,
which wandered the landscape searching for plants
to eat. At the front of its jaws was a sharp beak
used to bite off mouthfuls of tough plants, which
were then chewed with the broad teeth farther
back in the jaws.

Safe from enemies

In this Late Cretaceous scene in what is now
North America, a *Triceratops* browses on low-
growing plants. An early type of marsupial
mammal, *Palaeoryctes* perches on a fallen
tree trunk. Nearby some predatory dinosaurs,
Albertosaurus search for prey. They would probably
prefer easier victims than *Triceratops*, which is
heavily armored against attack.
If threatened, it could have
charged toward its
enemy with its sharp
horns held low, like a
giant rhinoceros.

Triceratops

Locking horns

Male *Triceratops* dinosaurs may
have used their horns in ferocious
battles between rival males—just
like male deer today lock their
branched antlers in battle. The
male dinosaurs may have fought
for leadership of the herd and the
right to mate with females at the
start of the breeding season. They
may have locked horns and pushed
against one another with their large
bony neck frills (below). The
struggle would have continued
until one of the dinosaurs gave
in or was pushed to the ground.

**Triceratops lock
horns**

Albertosaurus

Protection or display?

Triceratops moved on all fours. Its legs were thick and strong to support its great weight, and its toes were spread out to help support their weight. There were five toes on the front feet and four on the back. *Triceratops* was not a fast-moving dinosaur, and if in danger probably stood its ground and relied on its body armor for protection. But the bony neck frill may have had another purpose. It may have been covered with colorful markings that could have been shown off in displays to attract mates.

Lambeosaurus

Pushing against each other

The battle is nearly over

Skeleton

The huge skull of *Triceratops* measured more than 6½ ft. (2 m) from the nose to the back of the head. The horns on its brow measured up to a yard long. The neck frill at the back of the head was a solid sheet of bone and acted as a protective shield for the neck and shoulders.

Brow horn

Toothless beak

Defense

Just like animals today, dinosaurs had many ways of defending themselves from attack by predators. The largest dinosaurs, such as sauropods, were protected by their great bulk and could lash out against enemies with their long, heavy tails. Duckbilled dinosaurs found safety in numbers and traveled in herds, keeping the young in the middle. *Gallimumus* and other small ostrich dinosaurs were fast runners and could escape from danger by sheer speed. And other dinosaurs had special built-in protection such as horns or body armor.

Chasmosaurus

Another horned dinosaur, *Chasmosaurus* was also well armored. It had a pair of curving horns on its brow and a single shorter horn on its snout. The bony neck frill protecting its neck and shoulders was studded with bony spikes and knobs, adding to the dinosaur's ferocious appearance.

Centrosaurus

Horned dinosaurs such as *Centrosaurus* were heavily armored with pointed horns on the brow and snout and a huge bony frill at the back of the head. The neck frill, too, was fringed with spines. If it was in danger, *Centrosaurus* may have lowered its head and threatened its enemy with its sharp horns, just like rhinos do today.

Long sharp horn

Styracosaurus

This horned dinosaur had a huge nose horn and an array of tall spikes around its neck frill. Most attackers would have been deterred by just the sight of *Styracosaurus* with its head held low to display its spikes. If *Styracosaurus* was forced to charge at an enemy, it could have ripped its body open with its pointed nose horn.

Styracosaurus

The sharp spikes on a stegosaur's tail were as much as a yard long.

Bony club

Euoplocephalus

Defensive tails

A dinosaur's tail could make a useful weapon. The tail of *Stegosaurus* was armed with sharp spikes that could cause serious damage when swung against an attacker. Ankylosaurs, such as *Euoplocephalus*, had a heavy club at the end of its tail made up of two large balls of bone. With the help of its powerful muscles, the ankylosaur could lash out at its enemies.

The ball of bone at the end of the ankylosaur's tail weighed 60 lb (27 kg).

Why did the dinosaurs disappear?

No one knows exactly what caused the mass extinctions that destroyed many of the Earth's creatures, including the dinosaurs, 65 million years ago. Some scientists believe that the dinosaurs may have been becoming less numerous a few million years before the final extinction. The drop in numbers could have been caused by the cooler climate that resulted from the many volcanic eruptions at the time. Other experts believe that the extinctions were caused by the impact of a massive meteorite that hurtled down from space.

What died and what survived?

Died

Ammonites

Pterosaurs

Dinosaurs

Plesiosaurs

Survived

Reptiles

Mammals

Amphibians

Insects

As well as dinosaurs, groups such as ammonites, pterosaurs, and marine reptiles **disappeared** for ever. Creatures that managed to survive the mass extinction included other kinds of reptiles, such as crocodiles, lizards, and snakes, as well as mammals, amphibians, and insects.

Meteorite impact?

A meteorite (above), measuring at least 6 mi. (10 km) across, may have struck the Earth at the end of the Cretaceous period and caused the death of the dinosaurs and other creatures. Huge amounts of debris thrown up by the impact would have darkened the skies for many years, causing a long cold period and the death of plants. Plant-eating dinosaurs would have soon starved to death, followed by the meat eaters that fed on them. The evidence for this theory includes the discovery of a vast crater near the north coast of Mexico (right) that could have been caused by a huge impact. Another important piece of evidence is the fact that rocks of that time all over the world contain minerals that could have come from a meteorite.

▲ This computer-generated image shows the meteorite crater now underwater and buried under a deep layer of rock. The blue area at the bottom of the picture shows the channel made by the meteorite as it landed.

Volcanic eruptions

Even a small volcanic eruption can cause local climate change, and in the Late Cretaceous there was an enormous amount of volcanic activity. These eruptions would have thrown huge quantities of ash and dust into the air, causing the climate to change and destroying plants and animals.

Volcanic eruptions that took place in the Deccan region of India at the end of the Cretaceous period caused a massive outpouring of lava. The lava formed the layers of rock now known as the Deccan Traps (above). They prove that there were extraordinary events on the Earth at this time that may have caused the death of the dinosaurs.

This scene in the area now known as Montana shows the effect of increased **volcanic activity** on the wildlife of the time. Debris has darkened the sky and blocked out sunlight. Plants are dying and with them plant eaters. Meat eaters manage to survive for a while by scavenging.

Quetzalcoatlus, a flying reptile (pterosaur)

▼Dromaeosaurus, a bird relative (maniraptoran) feeding on Edmontosaurus, a duckbilled dinosaur

Edmontonia, an armored dinosaur

Triceratops, a horned dinosaur

Pachycephalosaurus, a bonehead dinosaur

Fossils

A fossil is the remains of an animal preserved in rock. Hard parts of the body, such as teeth, bones, and scales, are most likely to form fossils, but fossilized eggs and droppings have also been found. A fossil may also be formed of an imprint in the ground, such as a giant dinosaur footprint. Fossils only develop in certain conditions. Imagine, for example, that a dinosaur has died on a bank of a river or lake. The flesh is eaten by scavengers and insects, leaving only the bones, which slowly sink into the mud. Over the years, more and more mud piles up over the bones. Water filters down through the ground, carrying natural substances called minerals. These turn the mud and bones into rock. The skeleton keeps its shape but gradually changes into a fossil.

These fossilized dinosaur **footprints** were discovered in Utah. Footprints provide clues about how fast dinosaurs moved and whether they traveled in herds.

The teeth in this fossil of **Eudimorphodon**, one of the oldest flying reptiles, are particularly well preserved. Their shape would have been ideally suited to grasping slippery fish.

HOW A FOSSIL IS FORMED

1 Most of the dead dinosaur's flesh is eaten by carnivores or other scavenging reptiles and the rest soon decays.

2 The dinosaur's skeleton lies on the bed of the lake and sinks into the mud.

3 Over millions of years, more layers of lake sediment are deposited above the dinosaur skeleton.

4 The land has risen and erosion has started to remove some of the rock above the skeleton.

5 Finally, the last layers of rock are eroded to reveal the fossil bones.

Where fossils are found

Land over much of the world is covered by soil and plants. But in deserts, such as the arid regions of Utah (below), or where a great flood strips away the soil, rock is revealed and ancient bones may be seen once more. Even then, only part of a skeleton may be visible in a cliff face or an area of excavation.

Teeth fossilize well and can reveal much about the lifestyle of the owner. This long sharp tooth would have belonged to a meat-eating dinosaur.

Discovering Dinosaurs

A sketch of *Iguanodon*, made by the British country doctor Gideon Mantell. He first discovered the remains of the dinosaur in 1822.

Most of what is known about dinosaurs comes from fossils, which may have been untouched for millions of years. Sometimes fossils are found by chance, but usually they are uncovered by teams of dinosaur experts called paleontologists. Before the fossils are moved from their rocky bed, a detailed plan must be drawn, showing the position of each one. This may help the experts reconstruct the skeleton. Once back in the museum, each bone is minutely examined for clues about the living animal. For example, tiny marks or roughened areas on the bone show where muscles were attached. Scientists also compare dinosaurs with similar creatures living today to work out how they may have looked and behaved.

Key
Fossil bones
Reconstructed bones

A reconstructed skeleton of *Baryonyx*

Rebuilding a skeleton

It is rare that a whole skeleton of a dinosaur or other creature is discovered. Usually missing parts have to be reconstructed with the knowledge scientists have of similar creatures. Only about 60 percent of the bones of the dinosaur *Baryonyx*, above and right, have ever been found.

An **expert technician** painstakingly removes the fossilized ribcage of an *Albertosaurus* dinosaur from its plaster cast.

An artist's impression of what *Baryonyx* may have looked like

Digging for bones

When dinosaur bones, such as this tyrannosaur skeleton in Alberta, Canada, are found, they must be treated with the greatest care. The bones are freed from the surrounding rocks by paleontologists who use tools ranging from chisels and pickaxes to soft brushes. Then the bones are encased in a layer of cloth soaked in Plaster of Paris. Once the plaster has hardened, the rock beneath the bones can be cut away and the whole section can be removed and taken to a museum laboratory for further study.

Tertiary Age

The Tertiary began 65 million years ago at the end of the Cretaceous, and after the disappearance of the dinosaurs. It lasted until 1.8 million years ago. It is generally divided into five shorter periods of times known as epochs—Paleocene, Eocene, Oligocene, Miocene, and Pliocene. During the Tertiary, there were dramatic changes in life on Earth. Mammals and birds became the dominant form of life—taking over from the dinosaurs. More and more types of flowering plants developed, and vast forests grew. Toward the end of the Tertiary, between five and two million years ago, the ancestors of modern humans first evolved.

Tertiary ecosystem

This early Tertiary scene in what is now Germany shows life around a lake. Huge tree-sized palms (*Phoenicites*), conifers (*Taxodium*), and sedges (*Caricoidea*) flourish. Primitive horses (*Propalaeotherium*) browse on the plants, but risk attack by crocodiles. Other mammals such as an anteater (*Eurotamandua*), a porcupine (*Pholidocercus*), a pangolin (*Eomanis*), and a bat (*Archaeonycteris*) feed on the many insects. Birds include the ostrichlike *Palaeotis*. The creatures shown here are based on fossils found in this area now known as Messel, near Frankfurt.

Palaeotis

Eurotamandua

Asiatosuchus

Troodon

The Tertiary world

Early in the Tertiary, Australia separated from Antarctica, and the Indian landmass continued to move north until it joined with Asia. The continents went on slowly moving into the positions we know today, and by five million years ago the world appeared much as it does now. North and South America became joined by a land bridge as sea levels fell.

North America

Europe

Asia

PACIFIC OCEAN

ATLANTIC OCEAN

Africa

EQUATOR

South America

India

Australia

Antarctica

Key to map

Ocean

Landmass

Sea-covered continent

Archaeonycteris

Eomanis

Propalaeotherium

Pholidocercus

133

Quarternary Age

The Quaternary, the most recent period of the Earth's history, began 1.8 million years ago and continues today. The first part of the Quaternary is known as the Pleistocene and the second the Holocene. The Quaternary began with a major ice age. Huge ice sheets spread south from the North Pole, and glaciers all over the world grew much larger than usual. So much water became frozen that sea levels dropped and land bridges appeared, connecting islands and continents, and allowing animals to move from one to another. The first humans date from the end of the Tertiary, but during the Quaternary humans spread around the world and modern humans, *Homo sapiens*, evolved.

Life on the steppe

In the Quaternary, the Russian steppe was home to herds of wooly mammoths as well as rhinos, giant deer, horses, and the ancestors of domestic cattle. Lion-type cats and human hunters preyed on these large plant eaters. Plant life was much the same as on today's steppes with grasses and small plants such as saxifrage and buttercups.

Wooly rhino

Wooly mammoth

The Quarternary world

By the beginning of the Quaternary, the positions of the continents were much as they are today. Since then, changes have been mainly due to climate as ice sheets have grown and retreated and sea levels have risen and fallen. The map shows the greatest extent of the ice sheets during the ice age.

North America
Europe
Asia
PACIFIC OCEAN
ATLANTIC OCEAN
Africa
EQUATOR
South America
INDIAN OCEAN
Australia
Antarctica

Key to map

☐ Ocean

☐ Landmass

☐ Sea-covered continent

Giant deer

Horse

Steppe lion

Glossary

ammonite A member of an extinct group of sea-living relatives of today's squid and octopus. An ammonite had a coiled hard shell inside which lived a soft-bodied animal with tentacles.

amphibian A four-legged vertebrate animal that can live on land and in water but usually lays its eggs in water. Modern amphibians include frogs, toads, and salamanders.

archosaur The group of reptiles to which dinosaurs and pterosaurs belonged. Crocodiles are the only surviving archosaurs.

Aves The name of the order to which birds belong.

beak A mouthpart made of horn on birds and some dinosaurs. Beaks are used in the same way as teeth to hold on to and to chop up food.

billion One thousand million.

Carboniferous The period from 360 to 290 million years ago.

carnivore An animal that eats the flesh of other animals in order to survive.

club moss A type of plant that lived before flowering plants and was most common in the Triassic and Jurassic. Club mosses were common in the Carboniferous period but are now almost extinct.

coprolite Fossilized dung or droppings.

crest A bony structure on the top of the head sometimes used to attract mates or warn off rivals.

Cretaceous The period from 146 to 65 million years ago.

cycad A type of cone-bearing plant that lived before flowering plants. Cycads had short thick trunks and long palmlike leaves.

evolution The gradual development of species of plants and animals through time. As plants and animals develop, or evolve, their characteristics change.

extinction The complete dying out of a type of plant or animal.

family A group of related species. For example, all the species of duckbilled dinosaurs, such as *Maiasaura*, belong to the family Hadrosauridae. The scientific name of a family usually ends in -idae.

ferns Non-flowering plants with finely divided leaves called fronds.

fossil The remains of an animal preserved in rock. Bones and teeth are more likely to form fossils than soft body parts. Impressions in mud, such as footprints, can also be fossilized.

ginkgo A tree that looks like a conifer but sheds its leaves in the fall. The only species of ginkgo that survives today is the maidenhair tree.

Gondwana An ancient landmass formed when Pangaea broke up about 180 million years ago. Gondwana split to form the southern landmasses of South America, Africa, India, Australia, and Antarctica.

herbivore An animal that eats plants.

horsetails Plants with upright stems and tiny leaves, which are related to ferns. Horsetails were very common during the time of the dinosaurs.

Jurassic The period from 208 to 146 million years ago.

Laurasia An ancient landmass formed when Pangaea broke up about 180 million years ago. Laurasia then split to form the northern landmasses of North America and Eurasia.

Laurentia The ancient landmass that consisted of what are now South America, Africa, India, Australia, and Antarctica.

mammal A four-legged vertebrate animal that has hair on its body and feeds its young on milk produced in its own body. Mammals include animals such as cats, horses, and humans.

mass extinction The disappearance of a large number of different species over a short period of time.

meteorite A lump of rock from outer space that enters the Earth's atmosphere and lands on Earth.

mosasaur A large, sea-living reptile, closely related to modern lizards.

order An order is a group of related families. For example, there are two orders of dinosaurs: the Ornithischia and the Saurischia. Some large orders are divided into smaller suborders.

Ornithischia One of the two orders of dinosaurs. The orders differ in the structure of their hip bones (see pages 40–41). All ornithischians fed on plants.

paleontologist A scientist who specializes in the study of fossils and ancient life.

Pangaea An ancient continental landmass that formed about 240 million years ago and included all the world's land. It later split into two parts— Gondwana and Laurasia.

Permian The period from 290 to 250 million years ago.

predator An animal that hunts and kills other animals for food.

prey An animal hunted by a predator.

Quaternary The most recent period of Earth's history, from 1.8 million years ago to the present day.

reptile A four-legged vertebrate animal that lays eggs with tough, leathery shells. Dinosaurs, pterosaurs, and ichthyosaurs were all reptiles. Modern reptiles include tortoises, snakes, lizards, and crocodiles.

Saurischia One of the two orders of dinosaurs. The orders differ in the structure of their hip bones (see pages 40–41). Saurischians included plant-eating and meat-eating dinosaurs.

scavenger A creature that feeds on the remains of animals that have died naturally or been killed by other flesh eaters.

species A term for a type of plant or animal. Members of the same species can mate and produce young that can themselves have young.

Tertiary The period of Earth's history after the Cretaceous and before the Quaternary. The Tertiary lasted from 65 million years ago until 1.8 million years ago.

theropod A meat-eating dinosaur.

Triassic The period from 250 to 208 million years ago.

vertebra One of the bones that make up a backbone. The backbone is made up of a number of vertebrae.

vertebrate An animal with a backbone. Mammals, birds, reptiles, amphibians, and fish are all vertebrates.

warm-blooded Describes an animal such as a mammal or bird that can control its own body temperature. Most reptiles and amphibians depend on the sun's heat to warm their bodies and are said to be cold-blooded.

Milleretta

Index

Note: bold figures show main references.

Lesothosaurus

141

Triceratops

List of abbreviations

Metric
cm = centimeters
m = meters
km = kilometers
km/h = kilometers per
  hour
km² = square
  kilometers
  kg = kilograms

Imperial
in = inches
ft = feet
mph = miles per hour
sq miles = square
  miles
lb = pounds

S

2 Peter Menzel/Science
useum für Naturkunde
ory Museum, London;
ry; 83 The Natural
numantha Rao/NHPA;
E. Caffi" Bergamo,
Museum, London;
nathan Blair/Corbis.

ger Stewart; 7 Steve
re Kirk; 12–13 Martin
k; 20–21c Steve Kirk;
on Girling Associates;
eter David
39c Steve Kirk;
Kirk; 54 Peter David
ncy; 56–57 Martin
51b Steve Kirk;

64 Peter David Scott/Wildlife Art Agency; 64–65c Steve Kirk; 65 Steve Kirk; 66–67 Steve Kirk; 68–69 James Field/Simon Girling Associates; 69t Eugene Fleury; 70–71 Steve Kirk; 72–77 Steve Kirk; 78–79 David Bergen; 80–81b Peter David Scott/Wildlife Art Agency; 81tl Peter David Scott/Wildlife Art Agency; 81tr Steve Kirk; 82–83 Peter David Scott/Wildlife Art Agency; 83 Elizabeth Gray; 84–85 Steve Kirk; 86–89 Steve Kirk; 87t Guy Smith/Mainline Design; 90 Steve Kirk; 90–91t Peter David Scott/Wildlife Art Agency; 90–91b Elizabeth Gray; 92–97 Steve Kirk; 98t Peter David Scott/Wildlife Art Agency; 98–99b Robin Bouttell/Wildlife Art Agency; 99tl Steve Kirk; 99tr Peter David Scott/Wildlife Art Agency; 108t Robin Bouttell/Wildlife Art Agency; 108b Peter David Scott/Wildlife Art Agency; 109t Peter David Scott/Wildlife Art Agency; 109b Steve Kirk; 100–103 Steve Kirk; 104–5 Steve Kirk; 106l Steve Kirk; 106–7b Elizabeth Gray; 107 Steve Kirk; 107cr Steve Kirk; 110–11 Steve Kirk; 112–13 James Field/Simon Girling Associates; 113t Eugene Fleury; 114–15 Steve Kirk; 116–21 Steve Kirk; 122 David Bergen; 122–23c Steve Kirk; 123 Steve Kirk; 123b Elizabeth Gray; 124–25 Steve Kirk; 126–27 David Bergen/Virgil Pomfret Agency; 126tr Peter David Scott/Wildlife Art Agency; 126cl David Bergen/Virgil Pomfret Agency; 130–31 Steve Kirk; 132–33 Peter David Scott/Wildlife Art Agency; 133t Eugene Fleury; 134–35 Jim Channell; 135 Eugene Fleury.
Side panel artwork: Michael Woods.